WORSHIP as Pastoral Care

WORSHIP as Pastoral Care

WILLIAM H. WILLIMON

Abingdon
Nashville

WORSHIP AS PASTORAL CARE

Library of Congress Cataloging in Publication Data

WILLIMON, WILLIAM H.
  Worship as pastoral care.
  Includes index.
  1. Public worship.   2. Liturgics.   3. Pastoral
  theology.   I. Title.
  BV15.W54   264   78-894

ISBN 0-687-46389-0

Scripture quotations noted RSV are from the Revised Standard
Version of the Bible, copyrighted 1946, 1952, © 1971, 1973 by the
Division of Christian Education of the National Council of Churches
of Christ in the U.S.A., and used by permission.

Scripture quotations noted NEB are from The New English Bible. ©
the Delegates of the Oxford University Press and the Syndics of the
Cambridge University Press 1961, 1970. Reprinted by permission.

The text on pages 142-43 is from *Informal Conversations with Seward
Hiltner* by Seward Hiltner and William B. Oglesby, Jr. Copyright ©
1975 by Abingdon Press. Used by permission.

MANUFACTURED BY THE PARTHENON PRESS AT
NASHVILLE, TENNESSEE, UNITED STATES OF AMERICA

To
My Students and Fellow Faculty Members
at
Duke Divinity School

The church is blessed through their competence.

Contents

Introduction

I never took a course in worship or the liturgy while I was in seminary. There were courses taught in this subject at my seminary, but it was the period of the frenetic, secular sixties, and I, preparing myself to be a pastor to modern come-of-age humanity, felt little need to spend my time thinking about something so anachronistic as worship. Besides, I was a Protestant, and what had things like the sacraments, liturgical prayer, and so forth to do with me?

But my first little church in rural Georgia taught me things that the seminary had been unable to teach. That little congregation of fifty or so members led me to worship even as I assumed that I was leading them! While the guiding images in my preparation for ministry were pastor, counselor, prophet, teacher, or administrator, my parishioners now thrust me into a new and infinitely more perplexing (and personally threatening) role—priest.

It was one thing to preach to them (and, at times, *at* them), to give them advice and guidance, to educate them and expand their knowledge of and practice of the

9

faith. All these pastoral activities could be done (or so I assumed) with a fair degree of distance, safety, and guarded involvement. Besides, there were plenty of secular models for these activities and much cultural approval for ministers who limited their roles to these categories.

But it was another thing to be their priest, to stand with them before God, to mediate between their lives and loves and the life and love of the Almighty. Even in this thoroughly rural, utterly Protestant, unbendingly nonliturgical congregation, there was no escaping the fact that I was their priest. They could call me preacher, and I could lead worship in my gray business suit, and we could sing gospel songs and have altar calls and testimonies, but there was no denying that I was their priest, the one who daily stood before them and God, leading them in their own liturgy whereby God could meet us and we could meet God. They confessed in their prayers on Sunday morning and with me in my office on Monday morning, and I heard their confessions and, in a myriad of ways, pronounced their forgiveness. They offered themselves and their gifts to God at the altar on Sunday and when they painted the Sunday school rooms on Saturday, and I helped them make and claim their offering as an offering to God. They shouted, doubted, sang, wept, saw visions, and shook their fists in rage, and, in short, they worshiped. And, I confess, in so doing they led me to worship.

There I was, astonished by their deep involvement in their acts of worship, perplexed by their unbending resistance to my well-meaning attempts to "improve" their worship, frustrated by their apathetic response to my most cherished values, surprised by their sometimes extravagant enthusiasm over my sermons and prayers that I had judged to be quite mediocre, swept into their unselfconscious moments of spontaneous adoration.

I became curious about worship. Why were they there

each Sunday? What were they doing, and what did they think they were doing? Why such intense anger, apathy, happiness, fear, and compulsiveness in their worship life? Why was *I* a bundle of reluctance and wholehearted enthusiasm, nervousness and confidence, self-doubt and celebration when I led them in worship? My curiosity led me to a study of worship and liturgy.

As I continued to think and write about the worship life of the church and as I continued to exercise pastoral responsibilities, I became frustrated with two aspects of my work as a pastor.

For me, pastoral care had been interpreted mainly in terms of pastoral counseling—and rather limited, carefully circumscribed models of counseling at that. I had learned various techniques and approaches to the counseling task, but many of these proved to be inadequate or unrealistic in an actual parish setting. The fifty-minute hour of the counseling session was more often the ten-minute crisis or the momentary sidewalk encounter. I felt that I was a conscientious, caring pastor, but, frankly, only a small portion of that care was devoted to "counseling" in any strict sense of the word. Besides, I was troubled by what I interpreted to be a growing cleavage between many of those who were in the pastoral counseling field and the theological affirmations and day-to-day pastoral work of life in the parish ministry.

On the other hand, I also experienced some pastoral frustration in my attempts to utilize in the church what I was learning about the liturgy in my graduate studies. While there was much ferment within liturgics and a great deal of intriguing change and new insights, most liturgical scholars limited themselves to historical spadework, theological reflection, or construction of badly needed new liturgical texts. As new forms of worship and new liturgical insights emerged, I experienced great difficulty in implementing these new forms

11

within the local church, and I saw that much more was involved in renewing the liturgy than simply educating the congregation to an appreciation of historically and theologically respectable liturgies.[1] Increasingly, I felt tension between my role as a priest who cares for and leads the worship life of the congregation and my role as a pastor who sees the needs, emotional attachments, and complex psychic forces at work in my peoples' lives, needs that I felt were bypassed or ignored by some of my attempts to ̄rejuvenate worship. Could I be priest and pastor at the same time?[2]

This book comes out of my own effort to better integrate the role of priest and pastor and to see some of the many ways in which worship and pastoral care can inform, challenge, enrich, and support each other. My goals here are to suggest some of the ways in which priests can be pastors and vice versa, to sensitize my fellow pastors to the rich resources for pastoral care within the liturgical life of the church, and to show how insights and skills of the pastoral care disciplines can be of service in the continuing task of liturgical renewal.

Chapter 1 speaks about the nature of worship and some of the liturgical presuppositions that undergird this study. Chapter 2 reminds pastors that worship has a caring dimension and that there is no true *pastoral* care that does not take place within the context of a worshiping, believing, caring, witnessing community of faith. In chapter 3 I seek to affirm some of the many ways in which the pastoral care disciplines can be utilized in a more integrative approach to our worship leadership. A specific psychological and psychotherapeutic insight is then utilized in chapter 4 to speak of the near and far of worship. The next four chapters are my attempt to examine some specific acts of worship and to speculate on some of their psychological functions and pastoral dimensions as an invitation to pastors to begin to think more integratively about worship and pastoral

care. In the last chapter I have some observations to
share concerning the one who leads the liturgy and
cares for the congregation.

My special thanks to my colleagues here at Duke
Divinity School who teach pastoral psychology and who
read this manuscript while it was in progress, Dr.
Richard Goodling and Dr. Paul Mickey. Thanks also to
my former teacher of pastoral psychology at Emory
University, Dr. Rodney Hunter. While these friends did
not agree with everything I said here and should not be
blamed for any inadequacies of this book, their
encouragement and advice were indispensible. Mrs.
Patsy Martin, my secretary, has rendered valuable
assistance in typing and editing the manuscript. My
students, former parishioners, and fellow pastors have
been the source of my case studies that are used here
with their permission and with my gratitude. I look
upon this book, therefore, as a kind of community
product—the community of faith, that is.

Carlyle Marney, my late colleague who once taught
future pastors with me here at Duke, was fond of saying
something to the effect that "our worship has to do with
who God is, but it also has to do with who we are and who
we wish to God we were!" What more could the one who
is both priest and pastor ask than to be the instrument of
that activity and insight among the people whom God
has loved, Christ came to save, and the minister is called
to serve?

I
Why Are We Concerned?

Pity the poor pastor. The pastor has borne the brunt
of an avalanche of criticism in recent years, has been
told that he or she preaches poorly to a conglomeration
of mostly comfortable and increasingly empty pews,
that the church is a doomed and decaying institution,
that he is ill equipped to do most of the things he or she
does, that much of what he or she does is of little lasting
consequence anyway, and that he is the proverbial
jack-of-all-trades and master of none. He has borne all
this amidst long hours, poor pay, and demanding
parishioners. Just before the pastor collapses into bed at
night, exhausted from the daily routine of visitation,
training, teaching, sermon preparation, recruiting new
members, church financial woes, and refereeing in
congregational squabbles, the pastor is told that he or
she must muster up deep concern for yet one more area
of church life—worship.

Why be concerned about worship? For many pastors,
worship is one aspect of congregational life that moves
along predictably Sunday after Sunday without too
much difficulty or criticism. Admittedly, few people get

uncontrollably excited in the worship services, but, on the other hand, few lay persons seem to desire change or innovation in the way worship is done; so, why tinker with it? Leave well enough alone.

For other pastors, worship is frankly not their chief interest. Many Protestant pastors would confess that they see their ministry chiefly in terms of pastoral care, teaching, counseling, administration, or social action but not in terms of worship leadership. "I tried doing some new things in worship," reported one young pastor, "but the people just didn't go for the changes. After a few unsuccessful attempts, I just gave up and decided to use my energy elsewhere."

Other pastors have given up on worship for different reasons. Having rarely had the personal experience of meaningful worship and failing to see evidence of worship as a meaningful event for members of their congregations, they have decided that worship must be a vestige from our premodern past that the faith can survive without today. The older forms of worship impress them as being curiously anachronistic, and the new attempts at worship innovation seem to be superficial. Therefore, worship is not their chief pastoral concern. Besides, how many Protestant pastors were told in seminary that worship leadership was the major task of the pastor? Our ministerial models were usually counselor, administrator, teacher, or pastor, but rarely priest.[1]

There are other lay persons and pastors who are concerned about worship. Indeed, it could be shown that there is more writing, thought, and change in Christian worship today than there has been in the past hundred years of church history. The worship of Catholics has changed more in the years since Vatican II (1962) than it changed in the past five hundred years. Mainline Protestant denominations that formerly spoke about worship as if it were no more than helpful

16

adornment for the main event of a thirty-minute sermon and altar call have done some fresh thinking, issuing a plethora of new liturgies, historical studies, and resources for liturgical innovation. Why such concern about worship at this time?

In his now classic work on worship, Paul Hoon admits that some of our motivating concerns for new wine in worship are mixed with the bad brew of some questionable values.[2] The Protestant cleric who used to look down on the manipulation and forced emotionalism of the old-time tent revivalist does not shrink from using modern liturgical gimmickry such as balloons, dance, clowns, drama, and contrived gestures of intimacy to induce various emotional states in his own congregation. "Anything to shake them up a bit," was the justification given by a pastor recently after subjecting his congregation to a forty-minute barrage of taped screams, slides of malnourished children, and his own "prophetic" sermonic scoldings. The use of worship for managerial ends and cheap emotional highs is not new in Protestantism. Utilitarian, pragmatic, motivational manipulation of people during Sunday morning worship is as old as Charles Finney's "New Measures" in revivals for prodding people down to the altar. As C. S. Lewis said, "The charge is 'Feed my sheep' not 'run experiments on my rats.' " When worship is reduced to a pep rally for the pastor's latest crusade or to a series of acts that contain the minister's own hidden agenda, our concern for worship is called into question.

Boredom with our liturgical ruts has led some of us into creative and innovative experiments that too often mistake liveliness for life and "lit-orgy" for "lit-urgy."[3] In typical American fashion, we assume that if people say that they don't get anything out of Sunday worship, that must mean that they are merely bored with the old and can be turned on with a "new and improved model"

17

that follows the latest style. Pastors frequently long for some new things to do in worship without questioning the source of their peoples' boredom and disengagement from worship or their own ministerial motivations for seeking the new. A second-century Eucharist would be new to most people. A well-led, skillfully interpreted, carefully structured worship service on Sunday morning in the traditional mode would be a radical innovation for too many congregations! Why do we desire newness in worship, and what form should that newness take? Are we substituting the experience of newness for the experience of worship?

Finally, some of our present concern undoubtedly stems from our basic Protestant free-church insecurity about worship. Having been nurtured on the watered-down, antiseptic grape juice of Protestant austerity, verbosity, didacticism, and staid middle-class respectability, we now find ourselves coveting the richer wine of fancier liturgies. Our worship seems so shallow, sterile, and contrived when compared to their worship. As one lay person remarked to me: "You just can't keep having revivals fifty-two Sundays a year. Something more has to happen." We envy what we perceive to be the security, self-satisfied identity, and priestly authority of the "liturgical churches" or the seemingly spontaneous exuberance of the Pentecostal and more radically "nonliturgical churches." Protestant seminaries, dominated for decades by pulpit-centered worship concepts and attenuated doctrines of ministry, neglected to prepare ministers for competent worship leadership. We were misled into thinking that the artful proclamation of the Word in the Sunday sermon was enough to feed a congregation for a lifetime. The burden of having to make worship happen ex nihilo for one's congregation Sunday after Sunday bears heavily upon the free-church minister. If the minister's efforts are on

18

target on a given Sunday, the congregation may worship. If they are not, the congregation flounders upon the minister's liturgical shortcomings. Too often our "Protestant freedom" in worship has left us free to wander aimlessly in the maze of our own liturgical ignorance and confusion. We reach out for something more.

In reaching for that something more in worship, we approach our best motives for a pastoral concern for worship. The question before us is not: Shall I innovate in worship? Shall we have more spontaneity or more formality? Shall I wear this black robe or that white alb? The most appropriate questions are: In what ways can I as a pastor help my congregation to worship? How can we help the people (for I remind you that *liturgy* literally means in the Greek "work of the people") do what they want to do on Sunday morning (worship God) but may not remember how to do? How can we as pastors use the resources in our tradition, in other traditions, in our pastoral care disciplines, and in new forms of worship to strengthen and edify our congregational life? Edification, upbuilding, is our chief pastoral goal.

In his monumental study of the ministry, Catholic scholar Bernard Cooke has shown that the chief task and ultimate goal of ministry in the early church was this edification.[4] The precise origins and nature of an ordained ministry in New Testament and patristic times remain obscure. But one thing is clear. From its earliest days the church set apart a few people for the task of edifying and nurturing the congregation and increasing its vitality and unity. All baptized Christians shared Christ's ministry to the world. All Christians shared the general ministries of witnessing, serving, praying, and evangelizing, but certain Christians had the specific ministry of caring for the congregation, guiding, sustaining, preaching, teaching, disciplining, and leading in worship. The ordained ministry is merely a function of the church. So far as we know, this was the only distinction between the *cleros* and the *laos* in those early times, and it continues to be the most important distinction today. All Christians share the common task of personally living faithful Christian lives in the world. The pastor has the additional task of helping in the formation and upbuilding of a faithful Christian community. The pastor's authority is received from God and the community, and the pastor's efforts are directed toward corporate concerns.

In their concern to fulfill their calling as upbuilders, pastors wisely turn to worship. Paul, in his exasperation with the smug factionalism and enthusiastic excesses of the congregation at First Church Corinth, reminded them that all their liturgical eating and drinking, praying, baptizing, glossolalia, and preaching had one goal: upbuilding. Paul told the Corinthians that Christian worship is primarily a corporate (and corporeal) affair; it expresses and forms the Body. If worship does not strengthen the community (the Body), it is not Christian worship (see I Cor. 1:2; 14:26). Karl Barth says: "It is not only in worship that the community is edified and edifies itself. But it is here first that this continuously takes place. And if it does not take place here, it does not take place anywhere."[5] If the community does not worship, it is not a Christian community. If worship does not upbuild and sustain the community, it is not Christian worship.

One reason that worship is the center of the Christian community's upbuilding is that in worship, all the community's concerns meet and coalesce. Just as Christ gathered individuals into his new body of believers around a table, just as the Spirit integrated diverse races and nationalities at Pentecost, so worship is always an integrative act of the community. Here word and deed, *theoria* and *praxis*, past and present, humanity and divinity, meet. The Israelites gathered in their tabernacle, their "tent of meeting" where they met God, themselves, their judgment, and their grace. All our worship must be meeting, *synaxis,* coming together. Most of the problems which we have created throughout the history of our liturgy were the result of accentuating one aspect of worship at the expense of other aspects. Is it not the essence of heresy to cling too ardently to one facet of the truth to the exclusion of other facets of the truth? Let this be a warning to us in our pastoral concern for worship. Worship is pastoral, edifying, corporate, and integrative.

Norms for Christian Worship

In focusing our pastoral concern for the worship of our congregation, might we be so bold as to ask, What is good Christian worship? James White has helpfully sorted out three norms for evaluating good Christian worship: theological, historical, and pastoral. In order to have Christian worship with integrity, these norms must find expression in our worship. Don Wardlaw has symbolized these three interrelated norms of worship in this "trinitarian" symbol:[6]

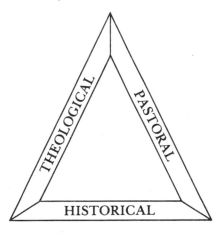

There is good theoretical justification for our adhering to these norms for worship. However, the main reason we are *pastorally* concerned that these norms be expressed is that we are convinced that these three principles make a difference in the lives of the people who are committed to our care.

To ask the *theological* question is simply to ask, What does our worship say about God? or the corollary, What does God say to us about our worship? Surely this is the toughest and most basic question to be asked, but, curiously, it is often the last question we ask. If we think about our worship at all, usually we think in terms of, What do *I* want from our worship? or, What do *my people* want from our worship? without daring to be so bold as to ask, What does *God* want from our worship? Is our worship the worship of the God of Abraham, Isaac, and Jacob; or is it the worship of Baal, Aphrodite, and Cupid? Does our worship have integrity when measured by the biblical standards for what our prayer and praise should be? So much of our worship is self-centered, mundane, and tame. How are we to be faithful to the gospel; how do we know the difference between secular idolatry and Christian liturgy unless we ask, and in some measure answer, the theological question?

To ask the theological question, to adhere to the **theological norm,** is not to drift off into vague academic abstractions. Rather, to be theologically concerned is to concern ourselves with some very practical implications of our worship. Christian worship rests on the assumption that it makes a difference how we speak and listen to God. The superficial silliness of many misguided contemporary attempts at "Celebration" and the dulled predictability of many traditional Sunday morning services may speak more to our adoration and protection of ourselves, our desires, and our notions than to the living God who calls us together. This is what Paul was saying when he admonished the saints at

Corinth: "When you get together you don't eat the Lord's Supper (*kurakon diepnon*), you are selfishly eating your own supper (*idion diepnon*) and you are eating it to your own destruction!" (see I Cor. 11:2-29). Perhaps, as Paul went on to say, one reason that we and our congregations are sick, one reason that our worship does not hurt or help and rarely heals, is that we do not worship the Wholly Other but only a limp, idealized image of ourselves. Too much modern worship has degenerated into a personality cult for the adoration of the preacher or a shallow narcissistic subjectivity that builds on the latest pop psychologies and fads.[7] We desperately need to recover the objective, transcendent, mysterious, prophetic focus in our worship. We need to turn again and worship God. "Let God be God in the Church!" Barth thundered in an earlier day. The theological norm reminds us that it is not so important *how* we worship as *whom* we worship.

The **historical norm** affirms that the manner in which our forebears in the faith spoke to God and were spoken to by God is of relevance for us today. It is no mere coincidence that liturgical renewal has gone hand in hand with the study of liturgical history. "Turn, return," cried the prophets of old when Israel wandered into faithlessness. They were not being antiquarians or nostalgia buffs, they were simply asking people to remember—and then to be instructed and judged by their memories.

Karl Barth once commented that what matters most in the church's worship is not up-to-dateness but reformation. To be *semper ecclesia reformanda* does not mean to go with the time or let the spirit of the age determine what is true or false. Nor does it mean to hide in the past. It means to carry out better than yesterday the task of singing a new song unto the Lord. "It means never to grow tired of returning not to the origin in time but to the origin in substance of the community." Or as

Pius XII said in his encyclical on worship, "To return in mind and heart to the well-springs of the sacred liturgy."[8] In our uniquely ahistorical milieu, sometimes the oldest truth has a strikingly contemporary ring. In our historical study of the liturgy, we are continually impressed by much that we have lost. Many of the liturgical innovations that were made during the heat of Reformation polemical battles have left Protestants with a truncated and limited liturgical life.[9] What was the early church doing when it celebrated the Eucharist every Sunday? Why did John Wesley speak of the Eucharist as the greatest means of evangelism and conversion? What were the pastoral concerns behind the medieval church's emphasis on confession and penance? Why has mysticism played such an important part in the lives of many of the church's saints? Why did the church come to insist on a public declaration of fidelity before it blessed a marriage? Those who do not know their history are doomed to repeat history's mistakes and to miss past glories in the narrowness of present expressions of faith. The historical norm reminds us that one of the best ways to arrive where we want to be today in worship is to first know where the church's worship has been before.

Finally, and most importantly for the theme of this book, there is the ***pastoral norm*** for worship. Christian worship should reflect the people who worship and the person or persons who lead worship. Liturgy is "the work of the people." We do not blush in admitting the thoroughly human character of this so-called divine service. After all, ours is an incarnational faith that rests on the scandalous notion that in the life, death, preaching, healing, and resurrection of a Jew from Nazareth we have seen as much of God as we ever hope to see.

The New Testament refers to the church as the Body of Christ. Just as the love of God for the world was embodied in Jesus of Nazareth (see Col. 2:9), so the love of God assumes flesh in the world through his church which continues to make God's love manifest in the world (see II Cor. 5:19 f.). To be sure, individual churches embody that love to varying degrees of adequacy; and yet, these overweight ushers handing out bulletins at the front door, these members of the Ladies Aid Society, these squirming pre-schoolers on the front pew, this elderly pensioner sealing his five-dollar tithe in the offering envelope, these new revolutionary missionaries in an urban jungle, this is the form in which Christ has chosen to be in the world.

So many times we pastors lament who these people in the church ought to be rather than understand who they are. We concoct "innovative worship" based on some theoretical principle of ours without seriously considering realistically the limitations and possibilities of our people. We limit our notions of what true worship is and fail to see when our people truly worship in their own way. We are baffled when they reject and resist the preconceived liturgical pigeonholes that we try to stuff them into. The pastoral norm reminds us to take the people who worship with pastoral seriousness and sensitivity.

In affirming the pastoral norm for evaluating worship, we are not setting our concern for people over against concerns for theological and historical faithfulness. I have often heard fellow young Turks in the clergy remark that "a pastor is just a prophet who has gotten soft." This remark assumes that prophetic zeal for the truth and pastoral love for one's people are mutually exclusive. Against this assumption I contend that our pastoral concern arises out of our theological and historical commitment and vice versa. When we worship, we worship a God who cared for humanity, who created an amazing variety of individuals, who entered our fleshly existence and thereby redeemed us.

25

Humanity has not looked the same since God became man. The nature of Christ determines the character of our concern.

Historically, and we will have more to say about this in the next chapter, the corporate worship of the church was seen as the principle sphere of pastoral activity and care. In administering the sacraments, preaching, anointing, blessing, and praying, the priest functioned as more than a divine/human intermediary. He functioned as the community's pastor dispensing means of grace through his liturgical leadership in the community. Unlike the Jewish temple cult or the pagan mysteries, early Christian worship was a family affair. It was more table fellowship than cultic ceremonial. To be the leader of the community's worship was to stand in behalf of and at the authority of the community and lead them in their table fellowship. The minister who helps feed people in the Eucharist on Sunday only repeats what he or she does throughout the week, nourishing and sustaining the flock as they live out their own ministries in the world.

On the other hand, to repeat an earlier statement, much of our theological and historical concern arises out of our pastoral commitment. In our American, anti-intellectual, ahistorical, utilitarian culture, many have the erroneous notion that such things as theology and history are mere cerebral diversions far removed from the arena of real life. Pastors are sometimes urged just to be with people, to "share your presence" in crisis situations without bothering people with theological niceties. The assumption is that a pastor's own personality is of infinitely more importance than his thoughts or beliefs about the faith or the community's fund of meanings. We will treat this in greater detail later, but for now I will just say in passing that one of my basic assumptions is that people are *helped* by refining their theological concepts and by enlarging their

26

cognitive understanding of the faith. Many of our personal problems have ethical dimensions. All of our human problems cannot be solved by merely getting our heads straight and thinking more clearly. But some of our problems stem from our misconceptions, our fuzzy thinking, our unexamined ideologies, our inadequate images, and limited notions. Any pastor who emphasizes subjective, purely intuitive, psychological, individualistic, so-called pastoral care of people to the exclusion of any reference to the more objective, theological-historical, and ethical context in which that care is exercised runs the risk of substituting some brand of secondhand secular therapy for Christian ministry. Our pastoral care is carried out within the context of a worshiping community attempting to live out its faith in this world. To forget that context in our care is to lose our perspective, our identity, and the source and resource of our care.

The purpose of this book is to focus upon one of our concerns as pastors—worship. Once again let us be clear that we focus on this particular concern, not at the exclusion of other norms or commitments, but rather in a desire to complement and inform our other concerns. I propose to use insights from such disciplines as pastoral psychology and pastoral and liturgical theology to sensitize my fellow pastors to the possibilities for significant pastoral encounters within our leadership of corporate worship. Psychological observations, theological perspectives, and case studies will be used as illustrations of how the various disciplines of pastoral care, when related to liturgy and worship, can provide a rich resource for our care of God's people.

Notes on Methodology

I am not a psychologist. For that matter, I am not much of a historian or theologian either. I am a

27

liturgiologist and sometime pastor. (I spend a fair amount of time writing, talking, teaching, and thinking about worship.) But because I am interested in worship, I find myself utilizing other disciplines in order to learn more about worship. I am forever being reminded of what a complex and multifaceted phenomenon Christian worship is. Specialization and detailed, circumscribed study may be adequate for other pastoral disciplines such as biblical interpretation or philosophical theology, but narrowness and limited focus are deadly to the study of worship.

The most effective pastors I know integrate tasks and perspectives. They do not wait until the board meeting is over to engage in pastoral care. They do not reserve worship for sixty minutes on Sunday morning. Seminaries took a step backward when they divided their curriculum into carefully defined departments and areas of study. The best pastors are generalists and integrationists because they recognize that all their ministerial disciplines are perspectives on reality; no one perspective has a corner on the truth or a monopoly on the ability to meet human need.

As we said before, worship is primarily a corporate and incorporating event, incorporating not only diverse people but also diverse traditions, expectations, expressions, and motives. This broad, all-encompassing nature of the worship experience frustrates systematizers and writers of carefully circumscribed books about worship; but, for the pastor, it should be seen as one of the best reasons worship must be central to parish life. Here, in that hour or so on Sunday morning, as well as at the funerals, weddings, and prayer meetings, our faith is expressed and formed, our innermost beliefs are transformed into outward acts and words, our past confronts the present, and our present leans forward into our future. Here, I wish to argue, we have a unique

28

opportunity to see ourselves and our parishioners in a new and revealing way.

As I said, I am not a psychologist. Yet I have found certain methods and perspectives from the psychological disciplines to be of great help in making sense of what goes on in our Christian worship. One of the things this book attempts to do is to use some of the tools of these psychological disciplines, within the context of liturgical theology, in a pastoral concern for the people who worship.

When I use the insights of pastoral psychology, my basic approach will be phenomenological. That is, I will take various phenomena of worship, looking for common themes in the way we describe what we do when we worship and lead worship, such as "priest," "pastor," "confession," "forgiveness," "sacraments," "matrimony," and so forth, and bring certain psychological thoughts to bear upon these subjects. Psychology, used in this way, becomes a kind of commentary, as Paul Pruyser says, an elaborate series of footnotes on liturgical themes.[10]

The danger in this phenomenological approach is that the natural cohesiveness and interrelatedness of the psychological concepts could be lost, in which ad hoc psychologies are applied to religious manifestations to the detriment of psychological integrity and unity. Conflicting psychological approaches might be applied differently to different phenomena. The result might be a series of superficial psychological observations with little cohesiveness or depth. If that is the outcome of this effort, I can only plead mea culpa and hope for others to undertake similar work with more skill. I openly admit that my chief aim here is not to be psychologically systematic, though I do hope to be pastorally consistent and faithful.

It first occurred to me that such perspectives as psychology could be helpful in a study of worship when

I found such perspectives helpful in studying myself. For instance, I like to think that certain theological and pastoral commitments determine what I do. But psychology helps to keep me honest by reminding me that my religious commitments are not as determinative of my behavior as I would like to think they are. In other words, psychology often exercises the prophetic function of telling me that everything I do is not done simply because I love God and the church! On the other hand, in a more positive way, psychology has also given me the graceful revelation that some of the odd and apparently meaningless things I do as a pastor often have ultimate, if usually hidden, meanings. Some of the things I think I do for myself are revealed to be faithful acts of beneficence. Perhaps Jesus was speaking of this mysteriously dual nature of our deeds when he said, "Inasmuch as you have done it unto the least of these, you have done it unto me." Remember, in the story Jesus told, how surprised the people were on the judgment day when they realized how they had stumbled on ministry unawares (or, on the other hand, how they had missed ministry in the inactivity)? "Lord, when did we see you?" is a question the pastor asks over and over in his or her mind as he or she goes about ministering.

The place of the pastoral care disciplines like psychology in this book is therefore viewed as a kind of commentary on the main event of Christian worship. I will try to let those disciplines speak for themselves but hear them as one whose principle concern is for the pastoral edification of the congregation through worship. Here begins a dialogue between the disciplines of pastoral care, practical theology, biblical and historical studies, psychology, and the liturgy, with the liturgy determining the ultimate significance of the conversation.

II
Worship as Pastoral Care

The popularly held assumption that *pastoral care* invariably means "pastoral counseling," with primary emphasis on counseling as a one-to-one psychologically-oriented encounter, has deepened but also limited the practice of modern pastoral care. In this chapter I hope to complement the recent efforts of pastoral psychologists like Don Browning, James Dittes, David Switzer, and Paul Pruyser, who have emphasized the *pastoral* dimension of our pastoral care, by my own effort to restore the *priestly* dimensions of pastoral care.

In their monumental work on the history of pastoral care, Charles Jaeckle and William Clebsch delineated four historic functions of pastoral care: healing, sustaining, guiding, and reconciling.[1] Clebsch and Jaeckle suggest that, while all these forms of care are present in the church at all times, because of changing circumstances, the Christian Church has tended to emphasize some forms more than others at various times in its history. For instance, during the period of primitive Christianity, in the church's first two centuries, pastoral care was characterized by an emphasis on sustaining souls through the vicissitudes of life in an often hostile world that Christians believed was running swiftly toward its end. Sustaining and supportive acts such as the Eucharist provided the community with the sustenance it needed to live in difficult times. For the next hundred years, as persecution of Christians by the state accelerated, many Christians, under pressure of persecution, fell away, or lapsed, from the faith. After this period, reconciliation of lapsed souls into the life of the church through acts of penance and contrition became a central focus of the care of souls. Another important shift in pastoral care occurred after the establishment of Christianity as a state religion by Constantine. Now the church was faced with the immense task of assimilating various groups into the ethos of the empire and the church. The catechetical lectures of Cyril of Jerusalem, explaining "the holy mysteries" of the church in step-by-step fashion to new converts after their baptism and Benedict's rules for monastic spirituality are examples of the kind of inductive guidance and discipline that went on during this time. In the medieval period, healing became an important function of the *cura animarum* ("cure of souls") mediated by the church's well-defined sacramental system that offered healing of maladies that beset any segment of the common life. Reconciliation to God was a prominent theme during the Renaissance and the Reformation. Later, the Enlightenment brought new pressures on the church to sustain souls as they passed through what the church considered to be an often treacherous and wicked modern world.

The "post-Christendom era" of post-Reformation, post-Enlightenment Christianity has presented pastoral care with a number of serious problems, many of which have their roots in the developments of society and the church in the last three centuries. The Enlightenment called the efficacy of the church's rites and sacraments into question. Healing, once the exclusive domain of the church (like education, social work, art, and so on), gradually separated itself from its ecclesiastical roots and emerged as an independent, secular activity. Newfound reason questioned the church's old formulas for personal fulfillment and individual well-being. Many souls were going elsewhere for their healing, sustaining, guiding, and reconciling. The revolutions of the late eighteenth and early nineteenth centuries brought with them pluralism and voluntarism which sought guidance that was educed from the values and norms of personal convictions rather than from the old, inductive guidance the church had offered before.

Likewise, the Protestant Reformation created a crisis in the care of souls. The source of the pastor's authority shifted from the nature of the church to the authority of the Bible or the leading of the Spirit. The identity of the pastor shifted from the conveyor of the sacraments and their healing grace to the one who is trained and called to preach the Word. The beliefs and practices of Protestant Reformers to the contrary, the sacraments in particular and public worship in general lost their place as chief loci of pastoral care in the churches that emerged from the Reformation.

The Protestant emphasis on the centrality of the Word, its concern with education, inner authority, and individualism made the Reformation, in part, complementary to developments within the Enlightenment. On the other hand, Protestant Pietism's stress on subjective feelings and personal experiential validation of one's religion tended to go against the excessive rationalism of the Age of Reason. Curiously, nineteenth-century Revivalism, which was particularly influential in American Protestantism, managed to blend many Enlightenment and Pietistic (and therefore

Puritan) themes. The theological stance for the modern age was set for Protestants by Fredrich Schleiermacher who declared in 1799, "The mission of a priest in the world is a private business, and the temple should be a private chamber where he lifts up his voice to give utterance to religion." Religion became viewed as a private, subjective, personal affair.

The results of the confluence of these movements are apparent when one looks at the dilemma of Protestant pastoral care. Clebsch and Jaeckle note that "the Reformation's great upheaval in doctrine and ecclesiology never generated a corollary revolution in the cure of souls."[2] The Reformation destroyed the Roman synthesis between speculative theology and practical guidance, between penitential piety and visible means of grace. It attacked the old calculus of sins and penances, stressing the radical nature of human sinfulness, the impossibility of salvation by works and the sovereignty of God's grace. But the Reformation inevitably produced its own brand of legalism, basing many of its norms for personal behavior (as Max Weber showed us) on the demands of emerging economic systems. Salvation became a commodity experienced by many outside the church, the sacraments, the community, and the tradition. The naked, solitary individual was left alone to make his peace with an often wrathful God.

Preaching, far from conveying a sense of Luther's gracious God, became synonymous in many people's minds with judgmental, paternalistic scolding. Pastoral care gradually became relegated to one-to-one dealings between the pastor and individual members of the flock. Protestant skepticism over the more exaggerated claims of late medieval Roman piety led to a deep distrust of *any* outward, priestly, ritualistic means of grace. The pastoral functions of sustaining, reconciling, and so forth, ceased to be, as they had been in earlier periods,

34

acts and signs done by the pastor for and with the community of faith and became almost exclusively thoughts, words, and feelings conveyed by the pastor to individuals. Many Protestants assumed that Luther's "priesthood of believers" (albeit in misunderstood, misinterpreted form) called into question *any* priestly acts on the part of pastors. *Pastor* became antithetical to *priest,* and the pastoral aspects of so-called priestly functions were overlooked.

The same could be said of the Reformation's effect on the practice of public worship. Liturgiologists have documented how the movement that set out to reform the liturgy; to transfer worship from the exclusive domain of the clergy and restore it to the people; to return Christian worship to its participatory, biblical, corporate, acted character; ended in virtually dissolving the sacraments, fragmenting corporate worship into private devotions, and relegating Sunday morning worship to a preacher-choir performance heavy with verbosity, didacticism, and moralistic scolding.

In an earlier time, a pastor caring for his flock, engaging in the activities related to the cure of souls meant, in great part, leading them in worship. There is much truth to the Jesuit liturgical scholar Jungmann's sweeping statement that "for centuries, the liturgy, actively celebrated, has been the most important form for pastoral care."[3] *Healing* meant anointing with oil, or unction, prayers to the saints and relics of the saints, and various forms of exorcism. *Reconciling,* pastoral care for the reestablishment of broken relationships among people and between people and God, traditionally meant those ritualized acts of forgiveness, confession, penance, and absolution. *Sustaining* meant administration of the Eucharist, confirmation, and other visible, concrete acts of communal support and divine grace.

A major difference in the pastoral care of previous ages of the church and that of our modern era is the switch from care that utilized mostly corporate, priestly, liturgical actions to care that increasingly limited itself to individualistic, psychologically-oriented techniques heavily influenced by prevailing secular therapies for healing, personal fulfillment, and self-help addressed to the needs of that twentieth-century creation, Philip Rieff's "psychological man."

Admittedly, earlier pastoral care was not exclusively a corporate, liturgically-oriented activity and may have been more individualistic than the existing documents show. John Chrysostom's touching "Letter to a Young Widow" and the *ars moriendi* ("the art of dying") literature of the Middle Ages come to mind as examples of personal, individualized, psychologically-oriented acts of pastoral care.[4] But in works like Richard Baxter's *The Reformed Pastor* an undeniable change of emphasis is evident. Discipline and strict pastoral guidance of individual souls are depicted as major concerns of the Protestant pastor. Baxter defines the two major concerns of the pastor in caring for his parishioners: "to turn the stream of their cogitations and affections, and bring them to a due contempt of this world" and "the evil of all sin must be manifested, and the danger that it hath brought us into, and the hurt it hath already done us, must be discovered."[5] Jonathan Edwards, the most creative of the early American theologians, first developed what was to be a Protestant concern for the next two hundred years: the investigation of personal religious experience and "affections." A century later, when William James's influential *The Varieties of Religious Experience* was published, James was only continuing a theme that Edwards had taken up before him: the delineation and validation of the great variety of individual religious experiences. James pioneered in the psychological study of religious phenomena and, as a pragmatic philosopher, emphasized the therapeutic value of religious experiences. But his *Varieties* also set the direction for the individualistic, pragmatic, utilitarian, psychologically-oriented nature of modern pastoral care.

A final touchstone in the development of the modern American Protestant pastoral care was the adoption, during the 1920s, of the medical model of pastoral care and the close methodological relationship between pastoral care and psychology. A key figure in this period was Anton Boisen, who, during his own hospitalization for mental illness, became convinced that the best method for training seminarians in the art of pastoral care was to expose them to people in crisis, the "living human documents" as Boisen called it. Freudian psychoanalytic theory was all the rage at this time (although Boisen was not a pure Freudian) and, at a time when American theology was in somewhat of a stupor due to the demise of the old Fundamentalism and the declining interest in the Social Gospel, Boisen's experientially based, "non-academic" approach to theological training was well received.[6] Clinical Pastoral Education (C.P.E.), as Boisen's training program came to be called, was a major part of the seminary curriculum in nearly every Protestant seminary by the 1950s. C.P.E. has primarily used medical institutions like hospitals and nursing homes as the setting for its work with seminarians and has relied heavily on medical, psychiatric, and psychotherapeutic techniques in its training for pastoral care. A generation or two of seminarians vividly remember their hours on duty as a student chaplain in a hospital emergency room, their often painful periods of personal reflection in a C.P.E. peer group, or their first encounter with sick, dying, confused, disturbed patients in the course of their clinical training. C.P.E. training has been of immense help as a means of enabling pastors and seminarians to better understand themselves and others.

But C.P.E. has been a mixed blessing in the training of

pastors. When the program has based itself in a mental hospital, it has often been criticized for training seminarians to minister to "abnormal" people in abnormal situations which do little to prepare them to minister to nonpsychotic people in normal parish settings. It would seem, however, that as a laboratory for learning, a hospital, prison, or mental hospital might be a good place to engage students in many demanding experiences in a short time. To me, the major criticisms of Clinical Pastoral Education are that it contributes to the current infatuation with pastoral counseling as the primary task of pastoral care and that its practitioners have not done enough careful thinking about the context of its care. In the C.P.E. setting, the primary models for ministry are often doctors, psychiatrists, psychiatric social workers, and clergy whose specialty is counseling and institutional work. The seminarian in C.P.E. moves about the hospital corridors sometimes even in a white coat—virtually indistinguishable in appearance, ideology, or terminology from the other health-care professionals. Psychiatric categories and terminology quickly are substituted for the language of faith. All problems become psychological problems rather than concerns for the *cura animarum*.

The majority of those who make up the American Association of Pastoral Counselors and the Association for Clinical Pastoral Education are specialists in counseling and institutional work and show, in my own dealings with them, an apathetic or hostile attitude to what they term purely academic questions of ethics, theology, and liturgy. C.P.E. supervisors, those who direct the clinical program in actual clinical settings, often show a keener interest in psychotherapeutic disciplines, counseling techniques, secular standards for pastoral effectiveness, and properly recognized credentials (a perennial problem for the pastoral counseling movement) than in some of the traditional disciplines of pastoral care. While there are those like Don Browning, Seward Hiltner, Thomas Oden, and Albert Outler who have done some serious thinking about the relationship between theology and psychology, they are not being read by many C.P.E. supervisors. The so-called dialogue between psychology and theology has been a mostly unilateral affair, with psychology doing most of the talking. I therefore agree with some of Urban Holmes's contentions that the Clinical Pastoral Education movement: (1) is lacking in awareness of the social dimension of human personality because of its fondness for one-to-one counseling situations, its continuing lack of prophetic sensitivity and its lack of appreciation for the positive effects of corporate structures. This leaves C.P.E. open to Thomas Oden's charge of being the last form of "liberal pietism"; (2) is implicitly anti-intellectual in its stress on feelings and emotions and in its apathy for theoretical constructs and hard thinking to back up its vast reservoir of gut-level experiences; (3) is related more in its identity to psychological than to theological commitments; and (4) makes pastoral counseling the chief function of ministry to the neglect of other basic ministerial tasks.[7]

I believe that Clinical Pastoral Education has been of great help in the preparation of men and women for ministry. My seminary training would have been deficient were it not for my own clinical work. C.P.E. has an undeniable effectiveness as an educational tool. In fact, many of the weaknesses within the Clinical Pastoral Education movement may be due to the fact that seminary faculties have handed over to C.P.E. supervisors nearly the entire burden of educating seminarians for the demanding, threatening tasks of pastoral ministry. But we must be honest about the limitations of this approach as a major emphasis in the preparation of pastors. The C.P.E. approach to pastoral care has a

39

definite relationship to the anti-intellectual, experiential, pragmatic, utilitarian, individualistic character of much of American Protestantism. The movement has been successful in capturing the interest and imagination of many seminarians and practicing pastors who have become dismayed and disenchanted with the vicissitudes of contemporary theology and fluctuating definitions of ministry. It makes ministry respectable to the church's modern "cultured despisers" and useful in the economy of modern, overspecialized technocracy which places great values on personal experience and on techniques for rapid personal growth (two values that have always been prominent within Protestant evangelical thought).

I am willing to concede that some of our criticism of C.P.E. and the pastoral counseling movement may be related to the fact that many of us lack the technical expertise and prestige of the professional pastoral counselor. I am also sure that there are many of us pastors who are always ready to lay hold of any available rationalization in order to repress and deny the deep challenges that C.P.E. and the pastoral counseling disciplines have brought to our ministerial roles, and, on the whole, I venture to say that more pastors and seminarians are excited by counseling than by liturgics!

In the next chapters, I hope to indicate how important psychological perspectives can be in helping us to see more in our ministry, particularly in the ministry of worship. In my criticism of pastoral care's tendency to reduce all pastoral care to pastoral counseling, I may be revealing my own equally misguided attempt to reduce all ministry to liturgy. Let the reader beware. But my own observations about the limitations of C.P.E. and its relationship to pastoral care appear to be confirmed by the emergence of a growing argument, coming from the pastoral counseling and pastoral care disciplines themselves.

The Worshiping Community as the Context
for Pastoral Care

In *The Minister as Diagnostician* Paul Pruyser of the Menninger Foundation asks in effect, "Why, in this age of widespread mental health services and available psychiatrists and professional counselors, would a person seek out a Christian pastor for counseling and guidance?"[8] Surely the full-time, professional, secular counselor has more training and experience in such matters than does a beleaguered parish pastor—even more training than parish pastors who may have done extensive work in counseling. Why, then, with the increased availability of resources, do they still seek their pastor in time of trouble? It is a rather simple question but one that I think more pastors should be asking themselves today.

Pruyser comes to this conclusion: "I believe that problem-laden persons who seek help from a pastor do so for very deep reasons—from the desire to look at themselves in a theological perspective."[9] They come, Pruyser argues, consciously or unconsciously to view themselves from the one perspective, to work out their problems in the one context, to set their needs within the framework of the one community that the secular therapist or counselor may not be able to give them—the community of faith and its ordained representative.

This strikes me as somewhat naïve and simplistic. I can think of many other reasons someone might seek a pastor for counseling or guidance: the desire for approval from a recognized authority figure and guardian of morality, the desire for available and free-of-charge counseling, and other reasons. But even given these possibilities, Pruyser is surely correct in urging pastors to take themselves and their unique context more seriously.

41

Pruyser contends that ministers must overcome their image of themselves as parapsychologists or as last resorts after secular therapies have been tried and failed or as referral agents for mental health professionals. This is not to deny that psychological and psychothera-peutic resources are pastorally and theologically appro-priate in the practice of pastoral care. The next two chapters will draw heavily on psychological and psychotherapeutic insights in the interest of developing more competent pastoral care and liturgical leadership. It is simply to remind pastors that they have resources that can help people, but they neglect their God-given, community-bestowed resources (Bible, liturgy, prayer, theology, community) in their misguided attempts to use only the resources of psychotherapy, pop psycho-logy, process management, and so on.

As an outside observer of pastoral work I am struck by the tendency of many pastors to neglect, overlook, or disdain certain classical churchly resources that are their professional heritage. Liturgical activities such as benedictions are often poorly performed. In pastoral counseling the allegedly correct psychological technique tends to be pushed so far that little room is left, in that pastoral fifty-minute hour, for the possibility of praying, scripture study, religious re-education, blessing, or prophetic confrontation.[10]

In this atmosphere, pastoral calling on parishioners degenerates into aimless chitchat for fear of intruding; pastors wait to be called upon for help, are careful not to appear to be judgmental or preaching in their approach to people's problems, and conceal themselves behind a façade of psychological techniques that are supposed to convey warmth and concern but that too often convey only detachment and impersonality. Are we wasting resources, Pruyser asks, that are psychologically justified (to say nothing of spiritually necessary)? When a person comes to his or her pastor, asking implicit or explicit theological questions,

42

how disappointing, then when his pastor quickly translates his quest into psychological or social terms, and fails to give him a theological answer! Or when he forgoes the opportunity for some religious re-education, from which the client may learn to raise better theological questions.[11]

A psychiatrist recently complained to me that, although he considers most of the emotional problems which he treats to have religious dimensions, he is frustrated to hear ministers talk only in psychiatric categories and language—and some of the most outdated, judgmental psychiatric language at that! Ministers thus fail to hear the faith issues behind the psychological distress.

Don Browning joins Pruyser in lamenting the neglect of pastoral resources in the practice of modern pastoral care. In *The Moral Context of Pastoral Care*, Browning chides pastors for adopting the Rogerian myth of "value free," "non-directive" counseling techniques with their one-sided emphasis on acceptance, forgiveness, and freedom without giving adequate attention to the underlying philosophy and the moral context of pastoral care. Part of the appeal of Carl Roger's "client centered therapy" was that it fulfilled the need that many felt in the fifties and sixties to find a pastoral identity that did not appear to commit itself to a particular theology, where moral judgments and "God talk" could be avoided in the interest of skillful listening. Browning feels that the earlier work of Hiltner, Williams, Oden, and himself was not so much wrong as it was one-sided in its emphasis. While Browning is mainly concerned about a new accentuation of the ethical context and the moral implications of our pastoral care, in a more general way he does suggest that, to deny the broader moral-theological-communal aspects of pastoral care is to overlook a significant source of people's problems and a basic resource for solving those problems and to send our pastoral care adrift on a sea of vague, unstated presuppositions and confused identity.

Browning affirms that there is a place in the church for pastoral counseling of all kinds—group counseling, one-to-one counseling, encounter groups—as long as they see themselves placed firmly within the context of the Christian community of faith and moral inquiry.

The minister has a clear duty to counsel the ill and dying, but he should first have helped create a community with a religiocultural view of the meaning of illness and death. Certainly the minister should counsel persons with marriage problems, sexual problems, and divorce problems, but he should first have helped to create among his people a positive vision of the normative meaning of marriage, sexuality, and even divorce. The difficulty with much of pastoral counseling today is that more time is spent discussing the tools of counseling than in the more challenging process of developing the structure of meanings that should constitute the context for counseling.[12]

While Browning's definition of the church (building on James Gustafson's definition) as a "community of moral discourse" strikes me as a bit limited and rationalistic in its focus, if Browning is being read by his colleagues in the pastoral care disciplines, one might expect a shift from the earlier Rogerian emphasis on one-to-one relationships between counselor and client to a greater appreciation for the necessity of community and its fund of meanings, from sporadic therapeutic dialogues to a continuing relationship with a community of faith that is often a therapeutic community, from the myth of value-free, client-centered techniques to a recognition that *any* method has an underlying ideology and ethical stance. If such a shift occurs, then we might ask the tough question, Is the ideology (theology) behind our pastoral care Christian?—a question we should have been asking long ago.

Admittedly, the world and the church have changed.

A cardinal sin of liturgiologists has been the lusting after some past age of liturgical glory (formerly, the Middle Ages, now, the pre-Nicean church) in which we were not bothered (we erroneously assumed) by creeping secularism or secular challenges to comfortable Christian formulas for human betterment. Exorcism, while of undeniable therapeutic value in treating illnesses of a thousand years ago, may be a questionable pastoral resource today. The old inductive approach to pastoral care had its weaknesses and abuses (moralizing, preaching at problems rather than confronting them, failing to listen, and failing to take seriously the complex nature of severe forms of emotional illness), and the Rogerians have spent a couple of decades making pastors painfully aware of their inadequacies as counselors.

But the medical model that some pastoral counselors have followed has its own weaknesses—too little emphasis on long-term sustaining and preventive care, some rather circumscribed definitions of *health* or *adjustment,* and its all-too-frequent smug professionalism which looks upon persons as things to be treated, clients to be dealt with rather than as people to be cared for.[13] We applaud writers within the pastoral care disciplines who have recently been noting that the psychological or psychotherapeutic models also have limitations. As we stated earlier, these models overemphasize the role of emotions in one's personal well-being without sufficiently recognizing intellectual, moral, and spiritual sources of human problems. In its earnest desire to become scientific (and therefore respectable), psychotherapy has tended to be most unscientific in the denominationalism and polarization of its opposing schools, in its refusal to be open to approaches that go beyond its own reductionistic conclusions, and in its earlier incessant labeling and pigeonholing of people and their behavior. Its individualistic nature has rendered psychotherapy unable to cope with the positive and negative effects of social circumstances. I am continually amazed at how many mental health professionals envy the freedom of Christian pastors to initiate contacts with people in crisis, to intervene in emotional distress, and to observe and be with people in a wider context of experiences than in the fifty-minute hour of a counseling session.[14]

Pastors have their problems in caring for the needs of people. We will speak in more detail about some of these problems later. But let us not exchange our problems for those of healers within the secular world. Of course, there are many doctors, psychiatrists, and counselors who are devoted Christians but who are not ordained ministers. This is something for the church to celebrate as an extension of Christian ministry in the world. But the ordained, pastoral healer has a particular function, a particular set of credentials, a particular responsibility—that of caring for and edifying the Christian community which is entrusted to his care (chapter 1). This makes it important for the pastor to raise questions that may not be the special concerns of those fellow Christians who have not been set apart by the community for these communal functions. It is important for pastors to use their pastoral/priestly identity creatively rather than to try to suppress that identity.

Not all counseling, even manifestly helpful counseling, is pastoral counseling. Pastoral counseling must occur within the context of pastoral care. And pastoral care encompasses much more than counseling—one-to-one or group counseling. We have seen that historically the *cura animarum* has been a multifaceted complex of pastoral acts directed toward congregational and personal edification and upbuilding (to return to Paul). The context, as Don Browning reminds us, is all-important.

There is no justifiable way of speaking about the care performed by the church unless one envisions this care in the *context* of an inquiring and worshipping church. The fundamental ambiguity of much that is called pastoral care today is exactly its tendency to perceive itself as an activity independent of or somehow not fundamentally influenced by this context. This is especially true of much that goes by the name of "pastoral counseling."[15]

The rootless ambiguity of attempts at pastoral care out of context are attributable, Browning thinks, to two reasons: (1) the rise of special pastoral counseling centers that often bear only a remote relationship either to the local church or to a larger denomination or ecumenical effort of the church, and (2) the fruitful but uncritical borrowing from secular psychotherapy as a resource for the church's pastoral care.

I agree. But while Browning focuses mainly on what he calls the "moral context of pastoral care," I wish to accentuate another aspect of the larger context—the liturgical context of pastoral care. My thesis is a simple one; so I will state it here: Worship is a major, if recently neglected, aspect of pastoral care. Worship can be enriched by a better awareness of the pastoral dimensions of so-called priestly acts. Just as pastoral care has often neglected the corporate context, so liturgical studies have frequently mired down in historical and textual trivia, archaism, and clericalism, forgetting the pastoral, people dimension in divine worship. In turn, pastoral care can be enriched by more attention to the priestly dimensions of so-called pastoral functions.

A warning note should be sounded here. As I indicated in the last chapter, the first and foremost *purpose* of our worship is to respond to God. In its most basic sense, worship has no other *function* than the joyful, ecstatic, abandon that comes when we meet and are met by God. Any attempt to *use* worship to educate, manipulate, or titillate can be a serious perversion of worship. As I noted earlier, much of our Sunday morning worship, especially in Protestant churches, has been flattened to a purely human enterprise in which people are the chief focus of our liturgy rather than God. While motivation for social action, comforting of grieving people, or education into a broader knowledge of the faith may all be worthy goals, if worship is viewed as only a technique of achieving these goals, worship is being used and thereby abused. God is not to be used for our own purposes, not even for our own good purposes. My thesis in this chapter is not that we should use the liturgy as a new method of pastoral care but that the liturgy itself and a congregation's experience of divine worship already functions, even if in a secondary way, as pastoral care. The pastoral care that occurs as we are meeting and being met by God in worship is a significant by-product that we have too often overlooked.[16]

In the New Testament, "worship" is a comprehensive category that describes a Christian's total existence. Liturgy is literally "the work of the people" whether that work occurs inside or outside the temple. We have, in our time, made too neat a distinction between *work* and *worship*. Likewise, Christian ministers, if they are doing what they have been called to do, will testify that no clear distinction can or should be made between their work as priest and their work as pastor. When the pastor counsels parishioners in his or her study, beside a hospital bed, or around a kitchen table, the pastor is only doing what he or she does in baptism, at the Lord's Table, in a sermon or a wedding—guiding the people of God in a liturgy whereby they are enabled to meet God and God can meet them. When the pastor breaks the Communion bread, raises his hands in a benediction, or leads in prayer, the pastor is only doing what he or she does in counseling or other acts of pastoral care—healing, sustaining, guiding, and reconciling those committed to the pastor's care.

Priest or Pastor: A Pastoral Incident

First, a little Bible study. In Reformation and counter-Reformation polemics the term *priest* came to denote an authoritarian view of church order, elaborate liturgy, and sacramental realism. The term *pastor* has connoted reforming zeal, strong ethical emphasis, and sensitive guidance and care for the "flock." Frankly, neither of these later consolidated and well-defined ministerial positions appears in the New Testament. There is no polarity there between the sacerdotal, "priestly" acts and the edifying, sustaining, guiding, "pastoral" acts. *Pastor* (that is, *shepherd*) only occurs once in the New Testament (see Eph. 4:11) although the verb for *shepherding* ("to tend") appears more frequently (cf. I Peter 5:2). Nowhere in the New Testament will you find the word *priest* directly applying to the Christian clergy although the verb meaning "to function as a priest" appears once (see Rom. 15:16). There are numerous places, particularly in the pastoral epistles, where sacerdotal or priestly functions are performed by ordained presbyters, deacons, and bishops (see James 5:14-16, I Tim. 4:14, Rev. 4:4).

It was once assumed that presbyters in the New Testament were mainly governing officials in the church, that deacons assisted in worship and carried out social services, and that the bishop presided in worship and exercised certain pastoral functions (in early Christian literature, *pastor* is used mainly to refer to bishops). At this early period there does appear to be a large delegation of various responsibilities. But any attempt to see clear lines of demarcation between our later clerical designations or any effort to show some political, theological, or functional relationship between our later designations of priest and pastor and the ordained ministry in the New Testament is doomed to failure. The picture is not that clear, nor are the

49

distinctions that definite. So-called priestly and pastoral acts were seen as interrelated aspects of the ordained ministry in general.[17] Perhaps we should learn something from this.

Setting: I was a student pastor serving a small rural church in Georgia. It was the first Sunday I administered the Lord's Supper. I went through the service as usual, but when I gave the invitation for Communion, only one or two members of the congregation came forward. Everyone else remained in their seats. After the service was over, a small group of us stood inside the church for a while visiting with one another. I could not contain my curiosity as to why so few people came up for Communion. So I asked the group: "Why did so few come forward today for Communion? Did I do something wrong?"

Incident: "I guess they just didn't think they were worthy to come forward today," responded one of the lay persons.

I asked him to say more about that. He then cited I Corinthians 11:29 about eating and drinking the Lord's Supper in an unworthy manner. As a pastor, this all struck me as a tragic case of misreading of scripture. I knew they had been told by some previous pastor that (to use the King James Version's translation of this text) this meant that if they dared approach the Lord's Table with unworthy thoughts or bad deeds on their conscience, they were "eating and drinking to your own damnation." I had come to know these rural people as deprived, beaten down, excluded by every institution in society—including the church where they were usually given "hell fire" sermons and devastating tirades. Here, in a symbolic, liturgical act, they seemed to be demonstrating their continuing sense of exclusion, self-degradation, and unworthiness.

"Let's sit down a moment, get out our Bibles, and look at this text," I suggested. Everyone opened his Bible, and we had a Bible study session then and there. I called to their attention that Paul says there was "immorality" and "drunkenness" at the Lord's Supper in Corinth. He was obviously dealing with a rather serious and extreme situation in which the Lord's Supper had been turned into selfish debauchery. Was this the case at our church? "No, certainly not," was the answer I received in return.

"Isn't the point of the Lord's Supper as we observe it that we *are* unworthy?" I continued. "We pray a prayer of confession at the beginning in which we admit to God and to everybody that we are unworthy. What are the words of invitation I then repeat?"

One of the women repeated the words from memory: "Ye that do truly and earnestly repent of your sins—"

"Yes! Doesn't Jesus eat and drink with sinners in the Bible? Didn't he say that he came to invite sinners? Maybe the only requirement for eating here with Jesus at his table is that you are hungry and know that you are hungry, and you believe that you can be fed here," I said.

We then talked briefly about humility, about false humility and the subtle pride some of them felt coming from those who take pride in the fact that they are so utterly unworthy to participate in the Lord's Supper—not like all those hypocrites who go forward at Communion! We noted that hypocrisy has many forms.

The next time we had Communion, I preached from Luke 5:29-39 on Jesus' meal at Levi's house. The sermon was entitled "Why Would a Good Messiah like You Be Eating with People like Us?" I also elaborated extemporaneously on the words of the invitation, attempting to stress the graciousness of

51

the event. Nearly everyone in the congregation came forward.

Reflection: I leave the reader to make judgments about my handling of this situation. I myself can think of other ways it might have been handled more effectively, in more depth, or without as much conceptual input on my part.

But for now, the questions I wish to raise are these: In this encounter, did I function as priest or pastor? Which of my actions were pastoral, and which were priestly? Priest, pastor, or *both*?

III
What's Going on Here?

In 1746 a pastor in Northampton, Massachusetts, by the name of Jonathan Edwards, noted what he called "surprising conversions" among his parishioners in the sweep of the "Great Awakening." Many Puritan pastors dismissed the awakening as mere mindless, meaningless "enthusiasm" to be firmly resisted or ignored. Edwards praised this new fervor in religion and defended it as "an Extraordinary dispensation of Providence." But he was not undiscriminating in his approval, for, as a pastor and a theologian, he saw disturbing excesses and "disorders" in this revival of religion. His own parish was soon split over the question of the validity of the revival, and a fierce dispute arose over who should be admitted to the Lord's Supper. It was out of this pastoral context that Edwards wrote one of his most important works and set the tone for American theology for the next two centuries: *A Treatise Concerning Religious Affections.*[1] Theologically, it was an attempt to answer the pressing question, What is true religion? Pastorally, the purpose of the book was to delineate the twelve signs of genuine piety and the rightly inclined heart. It both defended experiential religion and rebuked arrogant and censorious "enthusiasm." *Religious Affections* is a strikingly modern defense of the "affections" as the basis of religious assent and action and continues to be a classic in pastoral theology, a brilliant example of one pastor's attempt to give discernment and guidance to his people.

I have overheard seminarians making fun of the jargon they pick up in their C.P.E. training. The very mention of "What you are *really* saying is" or "Your *real* motive behind what you did is" is sure to bring forth peals of laughter from those who have spent time in the presence of clinical training supervisors. But this unfair caricature of Clinical Pastoral Education as a cliché-ridden, jargon-filled game of pseudoanalysis is not one that I wish to perpetuate here. Pastoral psychologists and counselors are rightly concerned with discerning real motivations, feelings, attitudes, and beliefs that lie behind or within or underneath (the location depends on which psychology you use) our surface behavior and false perceptions of ourselves. Such discernment is open to abuse when the analyst unknowingly reads his own hidden agenda into the analysis of another person's life or clouds what he sees with his own value commitments and limited perceptions. My psychology reminds me that I am capable of using nearly any tool, technique, or perspective in the service of my own defensiveness—including psychology! But the discernment, analysis, self-knowledge, and diagnosis that most pastoral psychologists advocate are indispensible tools for the pastor. They are biblically grounded in attempts of those like Paul who attempted to "discern the spirits," and they are historically related to the long history of pastors who, like Jonathan Edwards, struggled to "know thyself" as well as to understand the needs, sicknesses, misconceptions, and struggles of those who are entrusted to the pastor's care. To avoid the task of skillful diagnosis and analysis out of the fear of being an amateur psychiatrist is to avoid being a responsible pastor. Pastors, diagnosing, guiding, and discerning their parishioners and themselves by using the full range of pastoral skills and resources, are not being irresponsible, amateur psychiatrists. They are being mature, responsive, and responsible pastors. Psychological and psychotherapeutic skills and perspectives can be of great value to the pastor, as long as the pastor grounds the appropriation of these disciplines firmly within the context of the believing, acting, worshiping community called the church. From the church comes the pastor's credentials and responsibilities for diagnosis.

A guiding axiom for all study of human behavior since Freud has been, in the words of Seward Hiltner, that "all conduct has meaning."[2] This psychological observation is in itself an affirmation of faith in the essential orderliness and meaningfulness of human life. It is also an experientially validated fact of life. All behavior has meaning, however bizarre or capricious it may seem on the surface. There are times in every pastor's life when those words should be branded into his brain! How often are we perplexed and baffled by the apparently absurd behavior of ourselves and our people! Psychology forever prods pastors to "discern the spirits," a most valuable contribution to pastoral care.

Psychology also urges us to move from our clerical penchant for normative, judgmental talk about human behavior to a more descriptive, functional approach. There was much truth for pastors in Carl Rogers' assertion that the aim of psychotherapy is to let each experience tell its meaning rather than to distort experiences to fit previously assigned meanings.[3] In other words, we are urged first to adequately describe what a given action is and does for the person or group before we rush to judgments about the appropriateness of the action in religioethical terms. We are reminded that behavior cannot be taken at face value. There are layers of meaning and unconscious meanings that must be approached with some degree of analytic sophistication.

In my own seminary days I remember having the upsetting experience of preaching what I thought to be a rather mild sermon only to be verbally attacked after the sermon by one of the men in the congregation. He accused me of being "subversive" and "radical" and "ruining the church." When he had finally stopped shouting long enough for me to ask him to be more specific about how the sermon offended him, he cited two or three ideas that had no relationship whatsoever to my sermon, or at least my sermon as I intended it. I was hurt and baffled by what seemed to be my obvious failure to communicate clearly in a sermon and by my failure to relate to this man in the way that I had intended. All my attempts to state my points more clearly or to convince him that I had not meant to say what he heard were in vain. He stormed off in anger, and I was left with my confused frustration and hostility toward him because of his absurd outburst. Later, another parishioner told me that this man had a son about my age who had graduated from a fine eastern law school, who had been the center of all his father's hopes and dreams, but who had freaked out, joined a leftist group, and been arrested on several occasions for illegal activities. "Perhaps you remind him of how deeply his own son hurt him," the parishioner speculated. I did not have (or did not take) the opportunity to later probe the man himself, but I did feel that there was a strong possibility that his response to my sermon had deeper roots and more complex causes than who I was or what my sermon said. This

56

freed me to relate to him, not as an adversary, but as someone who, like myself, was entangled in a confused web of psychic stresses. In such cases, the tools of psychology can help us achieve transcendence of our situation, a perspective from which meaning begins to arise out of what would remain—without the ability to discern and to diagnose—meaningless.

Unfortunately, very little psychological reflection has been brought to bear on worship events. But I believe that worship offers the pastor a unique opportunity to "discern the spirits" and to answer the perennial, "What's going on here?" Some 75 million people gather for worship on a given Sunday morning in the United States. In most churches, that Sunday morning gathering will offer pastors the opportunity to see, be seen, and be with more of their parishioners for a longer period of time than any other activity of the church. While there, in worship, those people will probably act, think, speak, perhaps sing, respond, and feel in more complex, revealing, and significant ways than in any other activity of the church. Most of them go there voluntarily to receive and to give, to be with others, to be with themselves, to confront the faith and to avoid the faith, to be with God, and to hide from God. And always their pastor is there, functioning at their bidding (in spite of whatever he or she claims or denies) as their priest, leading them in worship.

John Carr, who teaches at Emory University, told me that at his former parish he had an early Communion service every Sunday morning. The attendance was irregular, with most people in the church coming to the eleven o'clock service. But the early morning Communion service began providing a place for parishioners to signal personal needs. Whenever John would see a person, couple, or family at that early morning service for the first time, his pastoral sensitivity would tell him that their presence might signify some special need they

57

had or some crisis they were going through. He therefore made a point to allow himself sufficient time to talk with people after the service, to allow them the opportunity to make contact with their pastor if they wished to do so. Time and again, the service became an opportunity for parishioners to alert their pastor to their needs (whether the parishioners consciously or unconsciously knew this was what they were doing), to seek pastoral care through their actions in public worship.

We are fond of one-to-one caring relationships. They have their place in pastoral care. But, in recent years, from the social psychology of Karen Horney and Harry Stack Sullivan to the dramatic social events of the sixties, it seems we have been made painfully aware that some of our greatest problems are group problems, "body" problems as Paul would say, social, political, communal problems. The one-to-one, fifty-minute pastoral counseling session in the pastor's study, too often has a safe, carefully limited, individualistic focus. Worship, I believe, tends to involve more risk, the risk of looking at ourselves within the context of the faith, the tradition, and the community that proclaims and lives by that faith and tradition and is judged by it. Worship entails the risk of transcending ourselves, of facing that Mystery that (as Rudolph Otto, and Moses, found) both repels and fascinates us, of standing on life's limits and asking life's ultimate questions. If all conduct is meaningful, surely our conduct before the Divine must have ultimate, special meaning for the Christian pastor as the pastor is both priest and pastor to God's people.

Motivation for Worship

If *liturgy* means literally "work of the people," if it is our work before and with God, then a psychologist might ask, What are some of the motivations behind

58

that work in worship? Paul Pruyser, in his *Dynamic Psychology of Religion,*[4] lists four motivational reasons behind the work that goes on in worship. First, we worship to *imitate,* on a small scale, ritualistically, what God does on a large scale, realistically. Paul said that we rise from the waters of baptism, repeating symbolically Jesus' rising from the tomb. We walk through the various parts of the Paschal event, from the upper room on Maundy Thursday to the cross on Good Friday to the Resurrection on Easter. Each Lord's Supper is an active remembering and redoing of the meal of Jesus. Medieval monks kept nightly vigils, lighting candles and praying through the nocturnal hours until dawn, unconsciously aiding the sun's return each morning. The early fathers spoke of the eucharistic bread as "medicine for the soul," claiming that special healing and nourishment came from the Eucharist. The priest anoints with oil and prays for the eradication of an illness.

The imitative and magical aspects of worship account for the high degree of precision and compulsion that tend to be present in the liturgy. Liturgical acts are invariably done in a careful, laborious, rigidly pre-scribed, exacting way. Any deviation from the detailed rubrics is thought to break the spell. A sloppy performance, an unorthodox (remember that the word *orthodoxy* means literally "right praise") mode of worship, a free rendition of the text, arc thought to bring the wrath of the gods. Liturgy tends to be viewed as being divinely ordained. Protestants are fond of calling their sacraments "ordinances," a fact that frustrates biblical scholars but that makes sense from a liturgical point of view. Nearly every Christian group will tell you that they worship the way Jesus did or the way they did in the early church. The texts, style, rubrics, clothing, actions, and music, are viewed as the specified terms under which the Deity will meet with people. By the way, the compulsion and precision are evident whether the worship is that of a so-called liturgical church or a nonliturgical free church. A Quaker meeting, a Pentecostal service, a Billy Graham crusade, all have a rigidly patterned, well-defined (if usually unwritten and unstated) order of worship. While some of these groups will claim to have no form of worship other than their spontaneous responses to the "Spirit's leadings," their participants know when someone is not doing it right or when someone has spoken out of turn or has said the wrong thing. Ultimately, there is no such thing as completely spontaneous or informal worship. True spontaneity and formlessness are virtually impossible to achieve in a continuing, worshiping community; to have such would be to fragment or destroy the community and the community-building functions of worship.

Another motive that Pruyser sees as determinative of the nature of our liturgical acts is *placation,* or *restitution.* When we have transgressed divine laws, there are acts by which we may restore ourselves: confession of misdeeds, postures like kneeling or prostration before the altar, gifts of money, the undertaking of some menial or difficult task to obtain restitution of guilt. It is interesting to note that, at a time when most Protestants and many Catholics have forsaken earlier methods of penance—Lenten self-denial, private confessions, and group confession and discipline—many psychiatrists and psychologists are advocating the recovery of confessional ritual and systematic acts of penance as being therapeutically useful.[5] Even in a church whose members appear to have dropped such practices altogether, one wonders how many of its members unconsciously look upon worship as a means of placating an angry God: "Even if I don't enjoy worship on Sunday morning, I feel better after I've gone, and I think it does me some good," or "I told God if he would

60

just get me through this sickness, I would be in church every Sunday."

Our worship also involves *commemoration*. The liturgical year with its round of festivals and seasons commemorates the great events of the faith and re-creates and renders contemporary those events. The same Protestant traditions that objected so strongly to the sacrifice of the Mass and its overtones of Christ's crucifixion redone in the Mass continue the same perspective with their definition of the Lord's Supper as a memorial, remembering and recreating the presence of Christ through the Table fellowship. Pruyser notes that whenever the commemorative aspect is emphasized, "one can expect a resistance to liturgical inventions; the commemorative work is a puristic attempt to recapture the original historical situation that is to be celebrated."[6]

Finally, a large part of liturgical work is related to *tribute*, giving God his due, breaking forth in exuberant praise to the Rock of our salvation. "Sing a *new* song unto the Lord" expresses the nature of tribute that tends to enhance spontaneity of action and freedom of form in worship. In even the most stilted and compulsively regulated worship, there are times for ecstatic moments and unplanned intrusions, when compulsiveness gives way to impulsivity, decorum gives way to warmth and fervor, inhibition gives way to release of physical and psychic energy. In fact, sometimes the most ordered and structured form of worship has the opposite effect of releasing the thoughts and energies of the worshipers for moments of free and unbridled adoration and praise. This is because predictability of structure and liturgical sameness enable the worshiper to participate without having to think about it, without having to worry about what is going to happen next; and therefore the worshiper is free to wander into the untrodden paths of praise and prayer. "Sometimes I just have to shout and sing" as one spiritual puts it. Tribute has a way of breaking the boundaries, of encouraging one to lose oneself: "lost in wonder, love, and praise."

These functional, phenomenological observations, while not exhausting the various meanings and functions of worship, should be enough to remind us that worship is a human activity, tied up with the complexities of human need and motivation. The activity we observe in worship is a basic, natural, human activity, observed in all cultures and societies. Anthropologists have found no culture without ritual, without public and private patterned ways of celebrating its values, passing on its norms, and creating a sense of its identity through imitation, placation, commemoration, and tribute. This seems true even for those manifestly secular cultures such as the Soviet Union. In worship, basic, fundamental, human needs are met. Too many pastors, expressing their allegiance to this or that theological concept, have run roughshod over these needs and have usually met with the hostility and resistance that people show when their needs are not being met and acts that have meaning for them are thoughtlessly disposed of. There are good, fundamental, psychologically explicable reasons why people react negatively when the satisfaction of these motivations and needs is frustrated by our "innovations." Many times our abstract concepts get in the way of our pastoring.

Of course not all work that occurs in worship has positive effects on the psyche. Worship can be a hindrance to the achievement of a healthy, mature, responsible, faithful personality. Sunday morning worship may create or intensify an authoritarian, judgmental climate in the congregation as pastors find themselves drawn unwillingly into situations that tend to foster images of the pastor as the resident demagogue, everyone's father or mother figure, or divinely ordained judge that may work against the pastor's efforts to free people for responsible, mature Christian behavior. However well intentioned, worship may reinforce destructive processes that are operative in a person's life. The prayer of confession may be used as passive behavior that keeps a person paralyzed, week after week, in self-justified inactivity rather than therapeutically freeing the person for renewed action.

Worship has long been accused, at least since the time of the Old Testament prophets, of promoting an escapist mentality. The prophets heard Yahweh say that he wanted "deeds of love and mercy more than burnt offerings." The ecstatic dimension of worship can be used as a way of removing ourselves from the demands and dilemmas of this particular time and place. The "sweet hour of prayer" can be used as an hour in which to reinforce our defenses, our denial, and to shore up our beliefs about ourselves and others, beliefs that sometimes need to be challenged. Freud documented the complex rituals by which we ward off relationships that are threatening and uncomfortable. Thus, while the stated aim of Sunday worship and its rituals may be *synaxis*, "meeting," it can also be a time in which we use a series of well-defined acts to avoid meeting God, ourselves, or others. Karl Barth underscored this ambiguous nature of our worship when he claimed, "Christians go to church to make their last stand against God."

These problems are not inherent in worship. They represent a misuse of worship or an unsatisfactory use of worship for psychic needs. Psychic factors are responsible for this misuse as they are responsible, at least psychologists would probably contend, for the misuse of all personal resources. The answer is not to discard the resource but to diagnose, to work with, and to understand those factors that interfere, block, distort, and pervert the resource.[7] Which leads us to the final concern of this chapter: pastoral diagnosis of the psychic, spiritual, and cultural stresses that may be functioning in worship.

Diagnosis in Worship

Worship, like all human behavior, has meaning. A person's selective interest in worship leaves clues concerning what is meaningful to him, where important centers of his emotional life are to be found, where his sources of anxiety lie, and how he deals with them. If we, as pastors, could learn to diagnose and analyze people's worship, here would be a rich resource of insight and revelation. Too often, our pastoral care reveals an active attempt on the part of pastors to guide, sustain, heal, and reconcile without first carefully diagnosing the problem. When we do engage in pastoral diagnosis, it is usually diagnosis of a largely intuitive and situational character. In the interest of providing pastors with a set of diagnostic guidelines that relate to the particular resources and needs of pastoral care, Paul Pruyser has devised seven variables that pastors might refer to in answering the question, What's going on here? While they are designed for use in what Pruyser calls the opening "diagnostic interview" of the pastoral counseling process, I see no reason why they might not also be applied to a pastor's diagnosis of a congregation's worship as well as the function and meaning of worship for individuals within that congregation. We have all seen sick congregations that represent, in group form, some of the same sicknesses we see in individuals. Aside from questions of therapy or treatment for diagnosed ills, our main interest here is to sensitize the pastor to the dynamics that may be at work in worship and to suggest some skills that will help a pastor in his or her pastoral assessment of worship. I will list Pruyser's variables and suggest some ways they might function in clearer discernment of the worship event. The suggested variables are not pointedly medical, psychiatric, or psychological. Pruyser has deliberately attempted to make them recognizable to theologians, capable of empirical verification, and able to span the richness and diversity that characterize religious problems. Traditional psychological words and jargon have not been used here by Pruyser because:

> I take a dim view of the diagnostic practices that prevail in psychology and psychiatry, and I see no reason for pastors to emulate them. All too often, diagnosing amounts to an act of mere labeling, of sticking a name onto something which makes one feign to know and understand it. Or it means choosing a word or phrase from a list purporting to contain classes of entities, with the implication that each class represents a solid bit of reality with clear boundaries between it and other classes, and that all classes together constitute the universe of entities for a given discipline. I am weary of the professional habit of summing up complex, fluid, and open-ended human conditions in one word, particularly when that word is a noun. Even more so when it is an artificial noun claiming prestige from pseudo-Greek and pseudo-Latin trappings.[8]

The first dimension of experience that Pruyser says we should examine is a person's *awareness of the holy.* What is sacred to him? What does he revere? Is there anything that is untouchable or inscrutable to him or before which he feels a sense of awe or reverence? To ask these questions is simply to ask, What does this person worship? Luther said your God is whatever you would sacrifice your daughter for. Tillich said "god" is that which concerns us the most, that to which we give our ultimate loyalty. Sometimes, when we gather on Sunday morning, we think we are worshiping God when in reality we are having a celebration of our material achievements, our musical and artistic sophistication, our moral self-righteousness, or our infatuation with the pastor! Pastors should be immensely curious about the gods of their people, not taking their God talk at face value but finding out what it really refers to as seen in their thoughts and actions.

A second diagnostic variable is designated by Pruyser as *providence*. What does a person's worship life say about his views about the disposition of the divine purpose toward him? "Why me, Lord? What have I done to deserve this?" are frequently heard questions. They are questions about providence. When a person is face-to-face with the mystery of God's presence, does he react as Isaiah reacted that day in the temple: "Woe is me!" or is his reaction that of Peter's at the mount of Transfiguration: "Lord, it is good that we should be here"? Do our prayers show a sense of trust, a basic belief in a larger, benevolent source of help, or do they smack of bargaining, pleading, and cajoling a despotic and capricious God into acts of goodness toward us? Do our petitions in prayer convey a sense that God owes us specific benefits, prompt solutions to problems, and magical aid; or do they refer and defer to a transcendent power that has its own unfathomable purpose that, although at times may be inscrutable to us, is a good purpose toward which all creation moves? Or has a person had no experiences in life that would foster trust and is therefore incapable of showing trust to God or anyone else? That timid, pitifully reserved, and self-contained soul who slips in after the worship service has begun, who does not seem to participate in any of the acts of worship, and who hurriedly rushes off at the conclusion of the service may be a person who, having previously found the world a frightening and untrustworthy place, now finds it impossible to risk participation and involvement because of fear of rejection. To ask, What is God's intention toward *you*? is to ask the question of providence.

A third diagnostic variable is *faith*. A person's

presence at worship and membership in a Christian congregation does not necessarily denote the subjective presence of faith. By *faith* Pruyser means a person's "affirming or negating stance in life." Where are the person's commitments? Are they enthusiastic or lukewarm? Does he embrace life and its experiences, or does he shy away from them? The popular lay characterization of Sunday morning worship as a "filling station" indicates the passive, wholly receptive way in which many people view worship. Many people come to worship to hear, see, and receive but not to give, act, or tell. In my own liturgical tradition, "altar calls" have been a traditionally popular occasion for response, commitment, and engagement within worship. The Eucharist, baptism, creed, and the offering are also times when one may affirm one's faith. Faith may be either a constricting or an opening experience for a person. To "hold on to my faith" may be the frightened response of an individual who lacks faith. One of the positive pastoral effects of change and innovation in worship is that it may invite or promote a greater sense of openness among the congregation. They may discover new and helpful ways of expressing and experiencing their faith. Persons' reactions to liturgical innovation can give a discerning pastor clues to their particular stance of faith. A show of anger on the part of a parishioner, as we shall see in the next chapter, may be a valuable indication of important faith commitments. Whether the faith is faith in the objective and historical tenets of the *Christian* faith is a matter for further pastoral investigation.

Grace is the fourth variable. The word *grace* has to do with gifts, generosity, giving and receiving. Grace is frequently tied to the theological concepts of acceptance and forgiveness. A person may be unwilling or unable to receive the gift of divine forgiveness because of the person's own feelings of unforgivableness. Behind persons' smothering sense of unworthiness may be their conviction that they themselves are the final arbiter of their condition and that no divine judgment or forgiveness is possible. A large amount of pride may be hiding behind their surface misery and self-loathing. I have noted the way that many worship services are heavy on the penitence and humility and light on grace and affirmation. "We are not worthy so much as to gather up the crumbs under your table" the Service of Holy Communion used to say. Sometimes the openness and the sense of dependence that grace requires of a person may be more difficult than continued self-centered wallowing in the depths of sinful despair. How many people stay away from church on Sunday morning with the claim that they are "not good enough to be a church member" followed by their claim, "But at least I am better than some of those hypocrites who do all that pious praying on Sunday morning!" The person who does not attend worship because "the church is not friendly" or the service is "cold" may be avoiding the worship because of that person's own sense of unacceptability or his inability to receive friendliness and warmth when it is offered. It takes grace to be able to participate in corporate acts like corporate worship.

Grace also involves the freedom to relate to the divine honestly and with the inner assurance that God is God *pro nobis* and will not destroy us because of our doubts, fears, or questions. The woman who claims to be "so thankful for the problems I have" may not be reacting in gratitude but merely in a cowering sense of fear. There is grace in trusting God enough to be honest about our hurt, our frustration, our anger at the workings of providence. How seldom do we let understandable human emotions like anger intrude on our worship services. For the psalmists, or for the saints of old, it was not so. "My God, my God, why have you forsaken me?"

is an honest cry of pain that is based on the gracious confidence that God is not threatened by our pain but graciously, tenderly hears our cry. The inability to express such feelings in worship, the inability to receive forgiveness and acceptance from God or from others in corporate worship, reveals much about the functioning of grace in a person's life.

A fifth variable is *repentance.* To repent means to change, to see oneself as an active agent in one's problems, and to be launched on a path of rectifying one's direction in life. Some of the first stages in what the psychotherapeutic literature describes as "working through" (integrating and appropriating new insights into subsequent behavior) can be seen in the acts of confession, forgiveness, and dedication that occur in worship. The pastor meets people who assume no responsibility for their problems, who present themselves as pure victims of circumstances beyond their control. The very activity and working through that occur in most services of worship challenge this passive feeling. On the other hand, the pastor also meets people who assume too much responsibility for their problems, whose consciences are overly sensitive to sin and blind to grace.

Of course, there is subtle prideful smugness to such overscrupulousness, the pride of being the "chief of sinners" which we mentioned before. I remember a sermon by Dr. Bill Muehl entitled "The Cult of the Publican" in which Dr. Muehl speculates on the popularity of Jesus' story of the Pharisee and the publican.[9] At first meeting, says Dr. Muehl, this publican with his great sense of humility and his cowering sense of unworthiness ("God have mercy on me a sinner") is most attractive—especially when compared to the obviously smug self-righteousness of the Pharisee ("God I thank thee that I am not like other men"). But after you have heard this story fifty or so

69

times, after you have heard the publican's humble lament over and over again, after you have seen him stop at the door of the temple a thousand times and refuse to go in because of his great sense of sin, you start to ask yourself: "Why doesn't he get on with it? Why doesn't he admit to his sin and then go on into the temple?" Muehl notes that there are certain advantages to the publican's humility. It frees him from having to change or decide or receive or act! Repentance is a dynamic process of awareness and action.

A sixth variable Pruyser lists is *communion*. Communion is close to the heart of worship. It involves the reaching out, the touching and being touched, the fellowship and sense of community that should exist wherever "two or three are gathered together" as Christians. The most basic aspect of communion is the person's disposition to see himself as one with the rest of humanity and nature. Is the person fundamentally embedded or estranged, open to the world or encapsulated, in touch or isolated, united or separated? In worship, a person may feel more painfully and more vividly than anywhere else his own sense of alienation and estrangement. For many people, this feeling of alienation is not their own fantasy; it is the result of conscious and unconscious efforts within the congregation to carefully differentiate between the acceptable and the unacceptable, the "we" and the "they." Because worship functions as a place of sharing, defining, and celebrating a group's identity, those whom the group looks upon as mavericks or troublemakers will be treated literally as *persona non grata*. When such devisive and alienating situations occur, the pastor's response is most important. It will be important for the pastor to uncover the various dynamics within the process of alienation and to avoid the trap of defensive argument and attempts to coerce the group or the individual from alienation to communion. Compassion may be called for in some cases, sharp confrontation in others. It all depends on one's diagnosis of the sources of the alienation and the potential for communion within the situation.

A seventh theme in pastoral diagnosis is sense of **vocation.** What is the person's or group's sense of purpose? What meaning is attached to their activities? Wherefore art thou come? is a question that needs to be raised before every congregation on Sunday morning. The line between work and worship, between the everyday, pedestrian details of the workaday world and the world within the liturgy, should be a thin and frequently broken line. Does a person have a sense of meaning behind his activities, a sense of mission and vigorous dedication; or are his activities, in the office or in the church, an aimless, listless wandering? The Sunday morning offering is a much-neglected opportunity to observe and enhance a person's sense of vocation. "That is *you* being placed on the altar, along with your gifts," Augustine said to his congregation. The offering is a time to claim work and its products as parts of the divine purpose of things, a time to view ourselves as important actors in the continuing drama of divine activity in the world. Does the person see himself as a participant, or as a passive bystander in the process by which the creation continues to be formed and loved? What do you think God is calling you to do and be today? is still a valid question, the response to which can give a pastor valuable insights.

A Pastoral Report

Situation: Jane, a young woman in my congregation, had recently been divorced. She continued to be active in the church during the period of her divorce except that she had dropped out of the choir. One afternoon, Jane came by my office and the following conversation took place.

Jane: Just stopped by to let you know how things are going.

Pastor: How are they going?

Jane: Great! Just great! The whole thing really hasn't been as bad as I thought it was going to be. I'm now looking for a job and have got some good leads. The kids are doing well, and I think we're coming out just fine.

Pastor: Good. I've been glad to see you at church each Sunday, and I'm glad your job prospects are good. But there's one thing I don't understand. Why haven't I seen you in the choir lately?

Jane: Oh, well, not for any big reason. It's just that I don't feel comfortable performing in front of people nowadays. Last time I tried to put on the choir robe and sing with them, I got so nervous and jittery that I just couldn't go out there. I thought I'd wait a few weeks before I try again.

Pastor: That's interesting. Do you have any idea why it makes you nervous to be in the choir?

Jane: It's just getting up in front of people.

Pastor: But I read in the newspaper this week that you had sung for the Women's Club meeting recently.

Jane: Well, that's different. I didn't mind that.

Pastor: I wonder why you were nervous singing in church but not at the Women's Club.

Jane: Well, the two are different. A lot of the people in the congregation think somebody like me shouldn't be in the choir.

Pastor: Has anyone given you the impression that they think that?

Jane: No. But you know how people are.

Pastor: I'm wondering how *you* are, Jane. I'm wondering if you're doing as well as you told me you are.

Jane: Well, it's no big thing. I'll be in the choir soon. I sure don't have anything to feel guilty about regarding the marriage.

Pastor: I notice that you used the word *guilty,* and I notice that you haven't mentioned *divorce.* Is what you're saying, "I shouldn't feel guilty, but I do feel guilty?"

Jane: I don't know. I'm sure that I have all kinds of feelings about the divorce. Sometimes those feelings crop up in strange ways.

Pastor: Like being nervous about singing in the choir?

Jane: Yes. I guess my nervousness should tell me something.

Pastor: Perhaps it should. Why don't you start looking at some of those feelings? You give me the impression that you may be going through more with this divorce than you want to admit to yourself.

Jane: Well, I have to get back in the choir soon.

Pastor: I want you in the choir. But more than that, I want you to come through this whole thing in one piece! I'm sure you can—particularly if you'll keep in touch with yourself, and us!

Reflection: Jane appeared to be burdened with many ambivalent, if unrecognized feelings about her divorce. As a pastor, I was at an advantage in talking to Jane because I had been involved in her divorce and because I knew a number of details about her that would not have been available to an analyst. (For instance, I knew that she had sung at the Women's Club.) Her anxiety, which manifested itself most strongly in worship, seemed a significant factor to me. Looking over the interview, it seems to me that I was doing much guiding of the conversation, frequently pulling Jane back to material that she tried to shrug off or avoid. At times, I think my guidance got in the way of her own self-revelation. My calling her attention to her use of the word *guilt* and her avoidance of the word *divorce* seems justified since these were her words. However, both her use of *guilt* and her avoidance of *divorce* may have been due to Jane's sense that I was leading her toward something that I, as her pastor, wanted to discuss, namely, her divorce and its moral and psychological implications, moving us toward a consideration of that diagnostic variable I have called (after Pruyser) "grace." It is interesting to note that she did use *divorce* after I used it, a positive response to my invitation to talk about it. Jane seemed to be experiencing judgment rather than grace when she worshiped. I have faith that the grace and forgiveness she seems to lack can come, but I think first she must receive the grace to be honest with herself. I believe some of that grace can come through the support and encouragement of the pastor and the congregation.

I selected this pastoral report as an example of how worship, when observed by using some psychological sensitivity, can be a revelatory experience of great pastoral significance, a vivid, expressive way of answering the question, What's going on here?

IV
Worship:
The Near and Far of It

I frequently receive inquiries from pastors who want ideas on how to innovate and do some new things in worship. My usual response is to ask pastors what is going on in worship at their churches each Sunday. The following reply is typical:

What happens in worship at my church—very little. I see an apathetic, dull group of people who go through the motions of worship in a lifeless, uncaring way. They listen politely to my sermons, then they mumble something vague to me about how nice the sermon was on their way out the door. The organist's attitude is "to hell with everybody else; I'll play what I want to and the way I want to." The choir is a perpetual battle zone of petty squabbles and hurt feelings, to be equaled only by the Altar Guild's fights. Few people speak to one another, except as they crowd into the rear pews. The youths look bored to death. The children squirm and giggle. The adults complain about any changes even while they yawn at the sameness. Something has got to be done to make worship more meaningful.

I agree that worship must be more meaningful. But in this chapter I argue that the first person who must find more meaning in worship is the *pastor*. I see the people's actions in worship filled with all manner of conscious

75

and unconscious meaning. Yet it is meaning that too often remains hidden to the pastor. The last chapter suggested some variables for diagnosis and discernment that attempted to take note of various psychic and religious motivational factors in worship. This chapter cites two interrelated psychological processes, approach/avoidance and resistance, and uses them as examples of how psychological observations can be applied to worship in a pastoral way. Sometimes we pastors do not see meaning in a given human phenomenon because we are looking for different meaning or are applying the wrong methods of discernment.

In *The Future of an Illusion,* Freud noted how religion often functions as an escape mechanism for a person, a way of escaping from the fears and frustrations in adult life to the protected, illusionary state of childhood.[1] Religion is thus a way of avoiding reality. Freud saw certain analogies between obsessional behavior patterns and religious rituals. Liturgy always runs the risk of becoming obsessively ritualized, rigidly rubricized, and neurotically patterned. The discipline of liturgiology has its share of Freud's obsessive-compulsive types who seem to have an excessive need to be proper, to "do it the right way," and to avoid any deviation from the pattern. The conflicting feelings of fear and love, attraction toward and shrinking from, the complex and compulsive ritualization by which the troubled person attempts to protect himself from his fears: all parallel activities and feelings related to the religious life. This was a helpful observation by Freud, particularly as it related to ritual and worship. But was this saying enough?

Jung did not think so. Of all of Freud's pupils, Jung has probably evinced the deepest and most sustained interest in religion.[2] Jung felt that all religions have certain focal points that give clues to humanity's conflicts and aspirations. Jung noted that religion performs a twofold function. First, religion provides an appropriate and culturally sanctioned means for helping persons get in contact with the "depths" of life. This was a function Freud did not adequately appreciate. Second, religion helps protect people from being overwhelmed by those depths through a patterned mode of approach and cultural limitations upon its presumptions. Freud had become preoccupied with the unhealthy, delusional use of religion to avoid reality and failed to see the healthy, creative, adaptive functions of religion as a primary means of dealing with reality.

When Jung looked at Western culture, he judged it to be increasingly out of touch with the depths, flat, isolated, and afraid to contact the *mysterium tremendum* principally because the West had lost the old primal symbols and rites that helped it approach and deal with the primordial mysteries and archetypal symbols. It had lost its "religious" means of approaching reality. A careless plunging into the depths without religious safeguards and "masks" might result, Jung warned, in severe mental disorder, not unlike the collective disorder represented by Nazism. When the church in Germany lost its once-powerful symbols and its well-defined ritual, it lost its means of helping people deal with the depths, with the ambiguities and mysteries of life. Hitler gave them symbols, rites, and experiences that enabled them to plumb the depths but with the violent and the demonic results of Nazi atavism and violence. What is needed, Jung argued, are ways to deal with the depths of life without destroying ourselves, ways of transcending the superficial without the violence that can occur when the depths are entered in a perverted or misguided way. I might also mention in passing one who was influenced by Jung, the creative historian of religion Mircea Eliade, who concluded that the function of religion, across all cultures and traditions, is sober and serious coping and adaptation.[3]

Eliade argues, from a variety of cultural perspectives, that religion, far from being a psychotic delusional flight from the real, is an honest attempt to deal with reality.

All this suggests that in worship we are participating in the twofold process of being brought into a relationship with the Divine as well as being protected from the Divine. E. R. Goodenough, following Freud, says, "Man throws curtains between himself and the tremendum, and on them he projects accounts of how the world came into existence, pictures of divine or superhuman forces or beings that control the universe and us . . . everywhere protecting himself by religion." Paul Pruyser suggests, with Jung and others, that the picture is more complex than that. The "curtain" of religion serves two purposes: It is a protective blanket, and it is also a projection screen. Like the veil in the temple that shields the divine mystery, it is a human instrument of protection that is also a background on which we paint pictures as a kind of ideogram of what lies behind that veil.[4] Our liturgy both conceals and reveals, protects and projects.

When we come in contact with the Divine, we experience ambiguous feelings of wanting to face the mystery and also of wishing to flee from it. The approach/avoidance pattern can be seen at work in many of our worship practices. The rite of baptism is spoken of in the New Testament as having the meanings of death, birth, rebirth, drowning, crucifixion, and cleansing. Baptism is thus a primal, earthy, powerful symbol of the mysterious, ambiguous forces in life and death. But if one witnesses the rite of baptism in many churches, it is reduced to a cute, sweet little ceremony in which water, with its rich and powerful symbolic connotations, is almost totally avoided, and the focus is on the cuteness of the baby rather than on what the liturgy says about the baby's sin, rebirth, death, and resurrection. It has thus become a tame, domesticated, symbolically empty rite in which we carefully avoid the early connotations. Even the incessant clearing of throats, whispering, coughing, rattling of gum wrappers, and aimless activity that usually goes on in a congregation on Sunday morning may be a direct, if unconscious, attempt to avoid getting too close to the mystery. Protestant clergy have been accused, somewhat ungraciously, of being infected with "diarrhea of the mouth" because of the constant chatter and irrelevant commentary with which they fill all empty spaces during Sunday morning worship. Perhaps their chatter shows their nervousness during times of quiet or unplanned breaks in the action of the service—times when the "numinous" has a way of intruding.

When attendance declines at a church on Communion Sunday, is it because people find Communion meaningless and irrelevant? That is the conclusion many pastors make about the matter. But the approach/avoidance syndrome may be operating here. Perhaps they stay at home and away from Communion precisely because Communion has meaning for them, but it is uncomfortable, threatening meaning. In the Lord's Supper, the congregation that is accustomed to Sunday worship in the form of sitting quietly in their pews and listening to the preacher, is now forced to act, move, kneel, eat, and respond in ways that may put them in uncomfortable situations. Of course, a pastor would have to probe this matter further using sophisticated curiosity and some of the diagnostic tools that we mentioned in the last chapter. But the approach/avoidance phenomenon reminds us that some apparent inactivity may be active withdrawal, meaningful response rather than meaningless apathy. We only avoid that which is threatening or frightening to us, that which touches us to the "ground of our being" as Tillich might have said it.

79

Resistance in Worship

Related to the approach/avoidance pattern is the psychological phenomenon of resistance. Resistance was first noted in the context of the psychotherapeutic process. How does the therapist explain that a person comes to him stating that he wants help with his problem, and then, as the therapist gets closer to the problem and its sources, the person does everything possible to avoid facing and dealing with the problem? The client may get hostile; he may accuse the therapist of being totally off base, of seeing problems where there is none; he may lie, evade, deflect, block, and use a wide range of resources to do everything possible to resist the therapist's attempts to help. The neurotic patient in psychotherapy is a bundle of conflicts: wanting to approach certain goals and yet afraid to do so, desiring to act yet unable to act, cooperating yet also resisting. Resistance in psychotherapy is thus defined as acted-out rationalization, a pattern of behavior that blocks or impedes the process of psychotherapy despite the patient's earnest motives to do well and despite the best therapeutic environment. Indeed, it could be said that one of the basic objectives of all psychotherapy is the meeting, examination, and possible eventual overcoming of resistance.

Psychotherapy's response to resistance should be of interest to pastors. Resistance is always seen as more than a bothersome obstacle or a meaningless hindrance. The resistance means that the therapy is touching or almost touching something that the client cannot yet handle, a result of intrapsychic conflict, something that provokes anxiety and therefore cannot be admitted into the discussion without either distorting or blocking it. In other words, the presence of resistance signifies to the therapist that the conversation has reached a potentially productive stage, an area of the psyche where the sources of a person's conflict lie. "Where there's smoke, there's fire," and where there is resistance, there is sure to be anxiety arising from some inner conflict. This should be of interest to pastors since I find that most of us look upon the various manifestations of resistance such as hostility, anger, disengagement, avoidance, denial, blocking, and so forth, as pastoral failures or as nuisances that must be suppressed or overcome. Psychotherapy tells us that such manifestations of conflict as resistance are intimately relevant to the important and troublesome themes of a person's life.

What does a therapist do when he or she encounters resistance during the course of a counseling session? The problem of the resistance is focused upon, with all the skills at the therapist's command as if the resistance itself were the crucial problem in the life of the patient. Similarly, the attention and the resources of the patient are invited to deal with the resistance. By not pressing what the therapist may suspect is the real problem and focusing instead on the problem of the resistance, the therapist indirectly indicates to the patient that he or she believes this is a manageable and discussable problem, not insurmountable and not beyond the patient's own resources for coping with it. By focusing first on the resistance—the anger, blocking, fear, hostility, and blaming—unrealistic fears can be recognized, their disruptive influence on the person's life can be demonstrated, and the patient can use these insights in future work on the source of the problem. Any attempts to ignore the resistance or prematurely cast it aside or see it as a meaningless obstacle to be overcome or attack it head on will usually be met with digging-in action on the part of the patient in which the resistance becomes more intense and more complex.

The resistance is merely the person's way of actively and creatively protecting himself from those truths or situations in life the person feels are so terrible, so overwhelming, and so tough that they are best kept safely tucked away within the depths of his psyche. Of course, protection is a good thing. There are truths and situations from which we may need to protect ourselves. But when our psychic protection mechanisms distort our ability to see our world and ourselves, when they rob us of our rightful share of the fullness of life and encourage us to retreat behind an increasingly fortified wall of fear and anxiety, that protection becomes our enemy rather than our friend. "You shall know the truth, and the truth shall make you free" may be a statement of eternal validity. But we must always be reminded that sometimes the truth hurts. Resistance is the psychological process by which we seek to protect ourselves from hurtful truth.

James E. Dittes, in his influential book *The Church in the Way,* suggests a number of ways in which pastors could use psychotherapeutic insights related to the phenomenon of resistance in their day-to-day pastoral care. The very title of Dittes's book is a summation of his thesis: So often we pastors look upon the withdrawal, hostility, conflict, and apathy that infect our congregations as meaningless obstacles to the tasks of ministry. In other words, the church often blocks, or gets in the way of, its own well-intentioned efforts to be the holy church by getting bogged down in human pettiness. But might these apparent obstacles be something akin to the phenomenon of resistance? If so, then pastors might consider another alternative to their usual ignoring or bulldozing of this resistance. That alternative would be for pastors to stop, to look upon the resistance as a valuable demonstration that something of great importance is being touched upon and as an opportunity to help guide the congregation in looking at and perhaps eventually working through (to use a psychotherapeutic term) that resistance. If the resistance could be dealt with in this manner, says Dittes, then the church that always seemed to be standing *in* the way of ministry might become the church *on* the way of ministry.

Dittes has an intriguing thesis. I can think of few patterns of behavior a minister meets more often than resistance. And, I think Dittes would say, for good reason. That church members frequently block, distort, withdraw, fight, and deceive does not necessarily indicate that they are a group of wretched sinners (they are of course a group of sinners—at least in the classical theological definitions of the church—whether they are *wretched* sinners or not depends, I suppose, on the details of your own ecclesiology). Rather, it indicates that the church has an admirable way of putting its members in touch with potentially painful, threatening, and anxiety-ridden truths and experiences, all of which will provoke various acts of resistance in people. The resistance is not necessarily a sign that the church has failed. It is more likely a graceful indication (though, like some other acts of divine grace, it may not seem so to the pastor upon first encountering it!) that the church is about its business. Resistance is an active, vigorous response that indicates not a failure of or obstacle to ministry but an occasion for ministry. Its presence shows that an individual can neither assimilate some act of ministry nor withdraw unto utter indifference.

As the church goes about the business of worship, resistance is sure to crop up. In fact, Dittes summarizes *The Church in the Way* by focusing specifically on resistance in worship.[5] If worship is looked upon as a problem by the pastor, Dittes says it is usually analyzed by the minister in one of two ways:

(1) The form of worship must be changed in order to make it more suitably matched to the needs of the people.

83

(2) The people must be changed and educated in the correct purpose, traditions, and meanings of worship.

Most liturgical reform and liturgical education begin from one of these two assumptions. To work from the first assumption often means that the pastor stoops to the level of the resistance, stops leading worship, and starts planning worship, becoming a rearranger of worship, tinkering with the liturgy, experimenting with something new, anxiously checking out the people to see if they like this or that worship style better than the ones before. If the second assumption is followed, the pastor moves from worship leader to worship educator. He or she constantly coaxes, invites, teaches, and tells about worship, assuming that if he or she can just get the people prepared, then they will at last be ready to worship. Either assumption may be appropriate. But Dittes notes that these assumptions usually distract the pastor from the actual task of leading worship by assuming that either the "objective situation" (the liturgy) or the habits, understandings, and attitudes of the persons themselves are the problem. Is not worship simply the active drawing near to God? Perhaps viewed from a psychotherapeutic perspective, the people are engaging themselves with purpose and direction in a meaningful response rather than in what the minister may think is a meaningless absence of direction. When we prematurely reject the people's response, we cut off the possibilities for meaning in this situation and cut off the people themselves. "The alternative is that the real feelings expressed in and by the resistance may also be captured and lifted up in the worship as important parts of the people who are placing themselves before God in their own way."[6] In other words, the pastor might continue to serve as priest, focusing upon the resistance as a part of worship, rather than forsaking the priesthood to become manager or educator.

John Bergland, who teaches preaching at Duke, tells of a young rural pastor who had been taught at his seminary that the worship service should begin with the people silent, humbly bowed in prayer, and in a "suitable" attitude of reverence. The pastor was continually perplexed by his little congregation's seeming inability to gather in silence. In spite of his hints and mild suggestions, they gathered on Sunday morning laughing, talking, and moving about the sanctuary shaking hands. Finally, one Sunday, before he began the service, he decided to tell them in no uncertain terms that he expected a more reverent and silent attitude on their part before the service. He scolded them, and they seemed to understand. Then, at the conclusion of the service, as people were filing out of the church, one old farmer went up to the pastor and said: "Let me tell you something. I heard what you said, but last night somebody told me that Joe's best milk cow jumped a fence and broke her udder. I knew that cow meant a lot to Joe and his family. They get most of their milk from her. So this morning, when I saw Joe and his family come into church, I got up and went over to where they were sitting and told him that after dinner I'd take one of my cows over for them to use. Tom then said he'd help Joe take his cow to the vet on Monday. Now when I got all that took care of, I was ready to worship." The young minister saw that, in his well-intentioned efforts to help people prepare to worship, he had missed their preparation to worship! Seemingly meaningless acts of resistance to worship are sometimes deeply significant acts of worship.

Fortunately for the young minister in this situation, he had a parishioner who was secure enough and articulate enough to help the minister make a better diagnosis of the situation. But such is not often the case.

Most of the time, the pastor must take the initiative to explore congregational reactions to worship, with the pastoral understanding that *resistance itself may be worship*. It may be inadequate worship or expressed in nontraditional ways or totally unrecognized by the very people who are engaged in it. But it is still a meaningful response to God, and that meaning is important. Moses' flight into the desert, Jonah's attempted escape from the mission to Ninevah, Paul's rabid religious fanaticism, could all be seen as meaningful, if not always adequate or successful responses to God in the form of resistance.

The practice of heading for the rear pew, like genuflecting, may be a habitual, expressive, and meaningful response to the situation of worship. It is a ritualized way of beginning worship. If the meaning of heading for the rear pew is different from that of genuflecting, there is all the more reason the pastor should try to understand it. Indeed, Dittes suggests that the person who invariably sits on the rear pew may know and feel more about what is happening in worship than the person who glibly trots down to the front pew. The person on the rear pew may be showing that he knows that he is coming before the Divine, and for that very reason he takes the rearmost pew. The clinging to the back pew may be more insistent and pronounced precisely on those occasions when the minister may plan an especially solemn worship service. This may seem paradoxical and irksome to the pastor but not if the pastor interprets these reactions as increased resistance to the increased worship stimuli. Chatting before the service, joking and playful activity during the service, the choir's loud shuffling of its sheet music, the Altar Guild's compulsive fussiness over the altar flowers, may be unconscious methods of distracting ourselves from the uneasy feelings that may result from coming into God's presence. The distractions may be expressions of how one feels about oneself in this context.

Of course, any or none of these feelings of awe or guilt may be involved in resistance to worship. They are suggested here, as Dittes suggests them, to point out to pastors that meaning may well lie behind such persistent and insistent resistance. It is not enough for the pastor just to personally recognize the visible signs of resistance and to hope that their meaning might be developed by the persons themselves. The pastor must respond and guide. He or she may use two main methods in responding when resistance is detected in worship: verbal reflection and behavioral reflection.[7] Verbal reflection may occur in conversations with individuals, small groups, or with the entire congregation, in which the pastor may find ways of expressing his or her conviction that even though this behavior may seem inappropriate, it is a meaningful reaction to the worship experience. Does the clinging to the rear pew involve feelings of alienation, exclusiveness, or rejection on the part of those who gather there? Care is needed by the pastor to convey the attitude that he or she wishes to give toward behavior. The pastor may note the behavior and simply say: "I wonder why this seems to be so persistent. Do any of you have any ideas on why our rear pew is so popular?" or the pastor may share his or her own speculation on the behavior. Such speculation can become perverted into a mild form of pastoral coercion, which may be appropriate if that is what the minister wants. But such verbal reflection can be a genuine form of acceptance and invitation to openness—which may be appropriate if this is what the minister wants.

For instance, in the first church I served, a conversation took place at the administrative board meeting that went something like this:

Pastor: I can't understand why people don't seem to use the bulletins I started printing. Every Sunday, after the service, they are scattered over the floor and pews. People seem determined not to use them during the service and still seem to want me to announce every hymn and go over all the announcements. I wonder what the problem is.

First Person: Maybe they just don't see the need of them. We never had bulletins before you came, and we seemed to get by all right.

Second Person: You know how folk are. They just like to do it the same way they're accustomed to.

Pastor: But I thought the church would be proud to have printed bulletins with a picture of the church on the cover. Then we could go through the service with no interruptions.

Third Person: It is too formal for some people. Some people think you ought to let the Spirit guide you in worship rather than plan it before you get here.

Pastor: Is that how you feel?

Third Person: Well, yes. Sometimes somebody might want to request a special hymn or want to make a testimony or something. How are you going to do that if it's all planned out?

Pastor: I see.

First Person: I think what she's saying is that the bulletin seems a little "citified" and cold to people. We are country people, and we like country worship.

Pastor: And the bulletins don't seem to fit who we are and what our church is?

First Person: Right. We've got people here who can't even read much. I'd hate to think how they must feel when we give them a sheet of paper first thing when they come in.

Pastor: You all seem to be saying that the bulletins are a hindrance rather than a help to worship. That's not what I wanted. Let's forget the bulletins from now on. Jim, I was interested in what you said about needing "country worship" for "country people." Could we do some more talking about what is special about our worship here?

A second approach to the resistance may be behavioral rather than verbal reflection as occurred above. Behavioral reflection might take the form of the pastor's duplication of the behavior that he or she observes among the parishioners in order to free them to reflect upon it with the pastor. For instance, the pastor might make a pointed effort to duplicate the parishioner's reluctance to begin the worship service on time. After a few weeks of late beginnings, the pastor might say: "I noticed how often I seem to run late in my preparation for Sunday morning. I never can seem to find my robe or my hymnal in my office. I always linger in the narthex visiting with you as you arrive. I wonder why? I've noticed that some of you seem to have the same difficulty in beginning worship. I wonder why?" This might be the beginning of a sermon or discussion in which behavior is examined, even though some might question whether such covertly aggressive behavior on the part of the pastor would elicit any more than defensiveness on the part of the congregation.

Sometimes the pastor, simply by his own behavior, may help the people explore with new sensitivity their own reactions to worship. A student of mine who serves as a student pastor was assisting his senior pastor in leading Communion on Sunday. During the Communion, one of the young men in the congregation fainted, hitting the floor very hard when he fell. "Keep serving the Communion, let the ushers handle it, act as if nothing happened," instructed the nervous senior pastor. But the student instinctively put down his tray of bread and helped the ushers assist the man out of the sanctuary. Then he returned and continued to assist the senior minister with Communion. What might the senior pastor's actions have told the congregation about

89

worship? To me, his behavior would have conveyed the impression that worship is a stilted, inhuman, cold, detached activity that cannot be interrupted by human need. The assistant minister's response would have said the opposite. I daresay many members of the congregation that morning had opportunity to examine their own reactions to worship by reflecting upon the different behavior of their two ministers.[8]

Worship can provide the communal context whereby behavior can be demonstrated, observed, reflected upon, and replied to within the service of worship itself. A pastor reported that he encountered resistance of his congregation to the use of a printed prayer of corporate confession. Most of the members seemed to prefer a time for individual, silent, personal confession rather than a public prayer. The pastor knew most of the theological and historical reasons a public prayer of corporate confession began the service, but he also knew that he had some of the same feelings as the people. He therefore added a time for silent prayer after the corporate prayer. But perhaps more significantly, he also preached a sermon entitled "My Checklist of Sins." In the sermon, he referred to the argument over which type of confessional prayer was more adequate. Then he confessed to the congregation that, when he went down his personal checklist of sins, he always dealt with personal, individual sins like bad habits, personal problems, and the like, and usually avoided the more corporate, communal sins in which he was a participant. Corporate sins like racism, overconsumption, sexism, nationalism, are some of our toughest sins and are ones that our personal piety usually avoids. "Forgive me," the pastor concluded his sermon, "but my checklist of sins carefully avoids my group sins. Let me continue to focus just upon my little personal habits. I have more control over them. Most of them don't hurt anybody except me. Don't force me to join with you and admit that your sins are my sins and that this is part of our general human condition, and therefore we are in need of general divine forgiveness. Help me keep my checklist carefully limited to what I can handle. Then I won't have to ask God for any help!" The sermon was followed immediately by a corporate prayer of confession that gave the pastor and the people an opportunity to confess some of those group sins. Here was a "confessional" sermon that became an invitation by the pastor to the rest of the congregation to join with him in reflection upon their shared resistance. The pastor's genuine curiosity can be a way of encouraging parishioners to analyze their own behavior.

Liturgical innovation is a frequent source of resistance. We have already suggested that the pastor's own motives for engaging in liturgical innovation may be open to question. Is our innovation an attempt on our part as pastors to avoid asking the more difficult questions about the sources of people's dissatisfaction with worship? We have also suggested that innovation definitely has its place. The innovation itself can be an invitation to the congregation to experiment with new ways of expressing themselves before God and experiencing God and others. The traditional "passing of the Peace" that has been restored by many liturgies as a time for the people to greet, touch, and respond to one another has had a mixed reception by many congregations. The idea of greeting one another in the middle of the service, much less physically touching, has often met with great resistance. But the Peace may be an attempt to invite people to do something that they may secretly wish they had the freedom to do. With time, and with pastoral guidance, the Peace has become a highlight of many congregations' worship. On the other hand, pastoral attempts at such innovative and potentially threatening acts as the Peace may be motivated by the pastor's not-so-subtle attempts to manipulate or coerce the congregation into the pastor's own preconceived form of "community." While diagnosing our congregation's motivations, we must also engage in the more difficult task of diagnosing the sources of our own behavior.

Resistance to such well-intentioned worship innovation can be a pastor's thorn in the flesh. But, this chapter suggests, it definitely can have its positive aspects. Resistance to innovation reminds the pastor that much is at stake in people's worship. What better argument for the centrality of worship in the church's life than the observation that it is the frequent scene of anxiety and tension? If the changes are aggressively resisted by the people, the pastor would do well to carefully reflect upon what the older forms mean to them. Resistance should also remind the pastor that liturgy is the work of the people. They, not the pastor, "own" it. A cardinal principle of the new liturgies is that worship must be given back to the people. Resistance may indicate that it is truly their worship, even if their participation in it and expressed ownership of it may profit from more satisfactory expression. The psychic skills that are required to sustain effective resistance in worship are precisely those skills that can also deepen one's encounter with the Divine in worship. The Divine is already engaging them in a powerful way, even if the pastor may wish their response to the Divine could be expressed in other ways. Above all, if the resistance is seen as an opportunity for pastoral care rather than as an obstacle to pastoral care, liturgical innovation can become a time for a variety of pastoral acts.

The nervous chatter and inane comments after a sermon like "A nice sermon, Reverend" may not denote, as pastors so often assume, that the point of the sermon was missed. These nervous reactions may be demonstrated proof that the sermon's point was heard and that hearing made the people uncomfortable. Sometimes the most effective sermon may not be the one that enables everyone to come out the front door and tell the pastor, "I remember your three points in the sermon and liked one but disagreed with the others." This can be a kind of rationalization that is more an avoidance of a sermon than a hearing of one. No, the most effective sermon may be the one by which people have been so touched or deeply moved (or angered!) that they may want to say something, but, rather than say anything to the pastor, everyone simply rushes out and heads for home. An apparent lack of response may be, in reality, a deeply felt response. As Kierkegaard once said, the test of a good sermon is not that you heard it, enjoyed it, then went home to Sunday dinner. The test may be that you heard it and found yourself too sick at heart to eat anything afterward! The pastor who is aware of that possibility and who is bold enough and cares enough to reflect upon the response within the psychological and spiritual dynamics of approach/avoidance and resistance, opens a rich resource for pastoral care.

An objection might be made at this point: How do we distinguish between a truly effective sermon that produces avoidance and resistance as opposed to a poor sermon that deserves only a yawn and nothing more? Have I simply given preachers another means for rationalizing bad sermons?

The objection may be well taken. It is entirely possible that a pastor may think that he sees a congregation's resistance to God or to an effective preacher when in reality, the pastor may only be receiving various kinds of negative responses that his poor preaching deserves. How do we know? There is no easy answer. Continual pastoral self-reflection, driving curiosity, and increased honesty will help. Just as the display of intense feelings, anger that is seemingly inappropriate to the situation,

93

or persistent deflection and blocking when confronted with certain facts may indicate a congregation's resistance to painful truth, so the pastor's own continual rationalizations, intense feelings, and persistent self-justification may also indicate the pastor's own resistance to some painful truth about himself or herself.

Another crucial question is, How can pastors know when resistant behavior expresses resistance to the Holy rather than resistance to something else? Not all resistance is religiously meaningful. How does one know if those rattling gum wrappers have to do with God or something else? If we define the Holy, as we suggested in the last chapter, as that which evokes awe, reverence, ultimate loyalty, deepest dread, and highest aspiration, then in one sense, people's experience of the Holy may be indicated by evaluating the intensity of their behavior—be it approach or avoidance. The display of surprisingly intense anger, fear, engagement or disengagement, bliss, or ecstasy, particularly when such behavior and emotion seem to be directed beyond both the pastor and the person displaying the behavior, particularly when the behavior seems to be unusually intense, may indicate that one stands in the presence of the Wholly Other. Of course, as was the case with that intense and ecstatic worship experience at Pentecost (see Acts 2), such behavior may be diagnosed as meaningless drunkenness rather than as the outpouring of the Holy Spirit. Sometimes pastors are in the same position as Peter was on that day, with a perplexed congregation, baffled by its behavior, asking, "What does this mean?" (Acts 2:12). On that day, Peter was able to affirm and help his congregation claim their unusual behavior as an encounter with the Holy, relating his "diagnosis" to the community's traditional expectations and beliefs concerning such encounters (see Acts 2:17-21) and his own pastoral intuition of the situation and his assessment of the consequences of such behavior (see Acts 2:43-47). Beyond these rather general guidelines, I know of no other infallible method for the pastor's "discernment of the spirits."

Finally, we must admit that a great deal of (perhaps most) resistant behavior that a pastor encounters in the church may be neither manageable nor soluble.[9] Resistance tends to be persistent, inevitable, and unconquerable in its personal and corporate expressions. Ministers will feel continuing frustration or else will develop serious delusions of their own power if they look upon resistance as something that can be successfully managed so that one can get on with the "real" work of ministry—changing people for the better. The common belief among many preachers that preaching changes people—at least, "good" preaching changes people—persists despite ample psychological, sociological, and theological evidence to the contrary. The belief that preaching (or for that matter, techniques of pastoral counseling, proper administration, good education, or expert leadership of the liturgy) changes people in dramatic and fundamental ways probably says more about a minister's frustration with human resistance to the gospel than about the empirically demonstrated effectiveness of these pastoral activities in changing people. We all want to manipulate one another, to have power over the lives of others; and the illusion that preaching changes people serves our needs. Even when we piously attribute the alleged effects of preaching to the "work of the Holy Spirit," this still often represents our desire to magically effect dramatic changes in people by virtue of our own power. Or it may represent the magical use of God's power for our own ends. And so people like me who write books on pastoral theology are forever aiding ministers in their illusion that if we just find the proper magic, preach more biblical sermons, lead more beautiful liturgies, or counsel more expertly, then people will be changed, our ministry will be "effective," and resistance, evil, and sin will be overcome. It is tempting to believe these illusions, but ultimately it is frustrating to base one's ministry upon them.

The psychotherapeutic principle of resistance reminds us of what we have forgotten in our faulty theological anthropology: that people do not yield to mere "facts," that resistance to the truth about ourselves and our condition is more persistent and more unconquerable than we think, that the "good we would do we cannot do." Acknowledgment of this fact of the human condition may lead us to recognize that we are dealing here with a problem that exceeds ordinary dimensions, that exceeds practicality, rationality, and morality, that is involved in the human condition as such. We are up against "principalities and powers," realities of an ultimate nature that are beyond our power, our techniques, our will, our understanding. In the words of Rodney Hunter:

The myriad resistances large and small that challenge, undermine, and frustrate our ministries at every turn are therefore expressions of the central human dilemma which ministry is all about and are not more impediments on the way to something else. Thus nothing short of a genuine theological understanding and a theologically informed ministry can be adequate in response.[10]

And what kind of response? To despair of our plight or to resort to magic and illusion would be to accord ultimate status to our resistance and thereby to worship the power of our resistance as being more powerful than the good purposes of God. A better way is for the pastor to identify with the resistance as *our* mutual predicament, as part of *our* human condition that *we* struggle against and sometimes transcend (but never succeed in overcoming completely), and therefore as indicative of our continuing need for God and for the mercy of God. Too much of our pastoral care theology is more anthropology than theology, and an inadequate anthropology at that. We therefore envision ministry as mere technique or expertise or method that certainly doesn't need the Cross or the empty tomb to make itself plausible to a humanity suffering under delusions of self-fulfillment, self-help, and autosalvation. A new realism, a new honesty about our common plight, coupled with a simple assurance of God's grace, may be more to the point of Christian ministry than all our efforts to change people for the better.

There may be no better answer, or solution, to the "problem" of resistance than to simply continue to praise God and ask for grace. Which is to say, we may not be able to do much more or much less than to worship.

I believe that the Bible says that the experience of coming face-to-face with the living God may be a pleasant or an unpleasant experience. It may provoke love or fear. One may wish to draw near or to run away. *All* these responses are part of the experience of meeting with and being met by God. Therefore they are all part of worship.

A Pastoral Episode

Situation: The minister had asked a number of people in the congregation to prepare to offer short prayers at a stated time in the worship service. One by one, each person stood where he or she had been sitting in the congregation and offered a prayer. All ages and all walks of life were represented. The prayers were simple, sincere, and moving. The entire congregation was visibly touched. Their prayers appeared to be a welcome change from the congregation's usually rather formal, restrained, impersonal service.

When the prayers ended, there were a few seconds

97

of awkward silence. The minister seemed to have been taken off guard by the depth of the prayers, seemed as deeply moved as anyone by them. The minister broke the silence by beginning to talk in fast, nervous, loud chatter which went something like this: "Well, uh, thank you for doing that for us. Now let's continue our service with the announcements. First, are there any visitors today? No visitors? OK. Well, everyone take up your bulletins, and let me call your attention to some important activities at our church this week—"

Reflection: The minister's talk about visitation and announcements seemed inappropriate at this rather sacred moment. Why was he leading the congregation *away* from worship rather than *into* worship? Why was he directly blocking this moment of divine-human encounter by turning the worship service into a civic club meeting?

This behavior seems meaningless until we view it from the approach/avoidance phenomenon. A minister is a priest who leads us before the Holy. But the minister is also a person among other persons who usually becomes uncomfortable when the Holy breaks in. The minister functioned here as our rescuer, the one who saved us from losing control, from getting too emotional, from getting carried away. Or did he save himself from these dangers? His behavior is understandable, given certain personal fears and needs as well as the cultural standards of white, middle-class society. But wouldn't it be helpful if he could focus upon that behavior? "I wonder why I responded that way?" he might ask. If that question could be asked and his resistance could be focused upon, he might get in touch with some of his own fears in the presence of the sacred, or with his fear of losing control or of not being the center of the congregation's attention, or with whatever fears lie behind his nervous, irrelevant chatter. And if those fears could be faced, then he might find himself free to face the fear next time, to recognize it when it occurs, and even to experiment with some new patterns of response like: "I feel like saying 'amen' to that! Let's all join in a hymn as we continue. Here's one that comes to mind." Or he might end with a spontaneous prayer of his own that sums up his and probably the congregation's bundle of feelings on such occasions. Knowing the truth, facing the truth, and accepting the truth about ourselves has a way of freeing us. It is that freedom of response with God and one another that we seek for ourselves as pastors and for our people.

V
Liturgy and Life's Crises: The Funeral

Liturgy functions as a means of helping us cope with life's most difficult circumstances. It helps us get by. "Ritual is part of a complex act of self-protection from destructive, unintelligible, and immoral forces."[1] By providing a patterned, purposeful, predictable way of behaving in the midst of crisis, by symbolically focusing our attention upon norms, beliefs, and sentiments regarding our ultimate concerns, religious ritual gives us a way through crises that might otherwise overwhelm us. Life crises such as birth, marriage, vocation, and death are accompanied by a complex series of rituals and liturgical acts. Generally speaking, the more threatening and potentially disruptive the crisis, the more detailed and carefully patterned the ritual that addresses that crisis.

The history of pastoral care shows two dimensions of the care of souls: (1) the preservation of spiritual health through preventive or protective care as well as daily guiding and sustaining care and (2) the restoration of spiritual and emotional health if and when dysfunction occurs through healing or therapeutic care. As we suggested earlier, the liturgy of the church can function within both of these dimensions of pastoral care. In this chapter we will reflect upon the therapeutic functions and pastoral dimensions of the relationship between liturgy and life's crises by focusing upon one of life's most difficult crises—the death of someone we love and the accompanying liturgical response, the Christian funeral.

Not too long ago, Jessica Mitford created a stir with her *American Way of Death*. In her rather simplistic denunciation of the American funeral industry, Ms. Mitford catalogued what every pastor already knows: that funerals are often an expensive attempt to avoid death rather than an aid in facing death, that many funerals are more pagan than Christian, that funerals are frequently characterized by tacky emotional insipidness, psychologically dangerous illusion, and monetary extravagance and exploitation. In the wake of Ms. Mitford's book came new interest in "private," "simple" funerals or unostentatious memorial services without all the ritual and trappings of traditional funerals. Many pastors, wondering if funerals sometimes did more harm than good and troubled by the apparently vulgar "paganism" of some of the funerals in which they were called upon to officiate, welcomed what appeared to be a deemphasis upon the funeral.

Funerals as Rites of Passage

But just as we were about to convince ourselves that the funeral was on its way out, social scientists, without any particular commitment to the funeral itself or to the stance of faith behind the Christian funeral, came forward with some firm convictions about the therapeutic and functional values of the funeral—encouraging pastors to take a second look at the funeral and to ask, "What's going on here?"

From anthropology and comparative religion came the image of a ritual as a rite of passage. Rites of passage are ritualized journeys across life's most difficult boundaries. They give meaning to the changes in the status or role of persons, they reestablish equilibrium in persons and communities after the crisis of change, and they serve the educational function of transmitting to future generations what the community believes to be the meaning of that change. Van Gennep looked at rituals related to such crises as death and saw three phases in these "rites of passage": separation, transition, and reincorporation.[2]

If we analyze the formal and informal rituals that surround death, we can group them around these three parts of a rite of passage. When a loved one dies, the bereaved experience a feeling of *separation*. The body is taken to the mortuary for preparation; the dead person is not there in his familiar chair nor at the dinner table in the evening; the living begin the painful process of separating themselves from the dead. Some psychiatrists feel that an important act of this separation process occurs when the grieving persons first view the body in the casket, particularly when many people die away from family and friends. While the mortician may have gone to absurd lengths to give the illusion of life to the corpse by the use of cosmetics, there is little doubt on the part of the family that the one in the casket is not fully the living, breathing one they knew and loved.

I remember a widow who, shortly before her husband's funeral service, asked me to go with her and look one more time at her husband's body. The coffin had already been closed, and I was reluctant to have it opened again, fearing that that might be a disturbing experience for the woman (and for me!). But she was insistent, and I consented. The casket was opened. She looked at her husband's body, touched his cheek tenderly, and said: "He's cold. You can shut it now." I sensed that the experience of physically seeing and touching the body had enabled her to proceed through the separation from her husband. "I just can't believe he's gone," she had said to me a short time before. Now she was starting to believe he was gone, a painful but absolutely necessary part of the process of grief. The rituals that surround the wake, viewing of the body, the graveside service, even the actual burying of the coffin, can all be visible, acted means of coming to terms with the separation of death. To avoid such separation is to postpone a necessary first step in the grief process and to run the risk of prolonging the pain of grief or dealing with grief in less productive ways.

The second part of the rite of passage that surrounds death is the process of *transition*. The person going through grief often experiences a time of limbo, betwixt and between, not living yet not dying. The world seems to stop. Appointments are canceled, time is taken off from the job, normal activities are suspended. The person is dealing with what anthropologist Victor Turner calls *limnality*, the ordeal of crossing one of life's "limits," of moving across one of life's significant boundaries. One day she is married, the next day she is a widow. One day he is a child with parents, the next day he is bereft of parents. Physical movement plays a significant part in transition: movement to the funeral home to select a coffin, the trip from home to the church or funeral home for the funeral, and finally the trip to the cemetery for burial.

During the transition activities, the actions of people within the community are important. At the time of death, a community often rallies in support of bereaved persons. Meals will be brought in; arrangements will be made. People who have experienced similar bereavement will offer advice and empathetic support to the grieving person. This relates to another aspect of the transitional phase of the rite of passage: education. Through the formal and informal rituals surrounding death, grieving persons are led into a new status. They are prepared for a new life status through the various educational functions of the rituals. I have noted the important role that widows in a church play when someone's husband dies. These women who have suffered the same kind of loss often support the new widow by giving her practical advice, drawing her into a new social group, and educating her for her new role as a widow. "It's not that bad," I overheard a widow comforting a woman whose husband had just died. "We girls take a trip every fall and spring and go to lunch together every Wednesday." She was attempting to help separate the new widow from those who are married and to educate her for her new status.

The funeral service itself has an important educative function. Here the church says in effect, "When death comes, these are things that we believe." The scripture readings, prayers, and hymns, all focus upon the values and beliefs that the Christian community uses to interpret the meaning of the crisis of death. The status of the dead is defined ("Blessed are the dead who die in the Lord" [Rev. 14:13 RSV]), the mourners are comforted ("Let not your hearts be troubled" [John 14:27 RSV]), and the living are instructed in the meaning of death for those who remain ("So teach us to number our days" [Psalm 90:12 RSV]). It is understandable that a frequently heard complaint at the time of death is, "I did not know what to say." The crisis, the mystery, the threat of death, lead to virtual speechlessness in the face of death. While speech can be used as an attempt to avoid the reality of death (i.e., our use of the euphemisms "passed away," "gone on to his reward," and others), and comfort can come from just standing beside a grieving family and upholding them with one's

104

presence; someone must speak. At some time some sense must be made of it all. Death must be placed within some meaningful, ultimate context. The funeral can be an important time for talking about things that, while difficult to discuss, must be spoken of.

Finally, there is the process of *reincorporation*. The mourners are separated from their loved ones who have died and are separated out for a time of special attention in which the community works in formal and informal ways to help the mourners make a painful transition. The final goal of these actions is reincorporation of the mourner into the mainstream of life. This is a crucial stage in the grief process. Will the grief be productive or destructive? Will the bereft person affirm the future or withdraw into defeat and despair?

The community usually has a number of ways of reincorporating grieving persons into itself. Friends will encourage such persons to get hold of themselves and to get back into things. Some churches have experimented with the formation of grief recovery groups which provide support to aid in reincorporation.[5] There may be an attempt to recognize mourners as people who need special attention and care. For instance, in most synagogues, mourners are asked to stand during sabbath services and on the first anniversary of a death in order that special prayers may be said. At the time of bereavement, many people report that their predominant feeling is: "I can't go on. I have nothing else to live for. My world has stopped." Through its subtle encouragement and prodding, a caring community tells the mourning person: "You can go on. You have much to live for. Life goes on, and you must continue to go on with life." Rituals in the church can help to keep people moving just as the resumption after a death of day-to-day rituals at home help the living to stay within the mainstream of daily life. As with any life crisis, the breakdown of daily rituals (getting up in the morning, grooming, going to work) often signifies emotional disruption and the struggle (or failure) to deal productively with the crisis.

Of course separation, transition, and reincorporation do not necessarily occur in rigid order nor in the span of a few days. Mourners may move back and forth between the various stages for many months, and one ritualistic act (the funeral service, for instance) may include elements from all three stages of the rite of passage. But all the parts of the process are important, and failure to complete one stage may make the completion of other stages impossible.

Viewing a funeral as a rite of passage is only one possible way to visualize how ritual and liturgy are related to a life crisis. But it is a helpful reminder that every life crisis provokes "dis-ease" and threatening disruption of a person's world. Before equilibrium can be restored, certain things must happen. New knowledge and understanding must be acquired ("How could God do something like this to me?"), new sensibilities and awarenesses may be called for ("God is upholding me in this time of trial"), and new skills and abilities will be needed in order to adjust and adapt to one's new status ("I must learn to get along on my own now"). In short, various kinds of socialization and education must occur. Liturgy is part of that education.

Psychological Insights on Funerals

From another perspective, the perspective of psychology, death provokes an identity crisis. When someone whom we love dies, part of us dies with them. Grief is the complex of emotional reactions that accompany this identity crisis. The grief we feel at the time of death may be related to our anger (How could she leave me after all I've done during her illness?) or to our self-pity (What is going to become of me now?) or to

106

our fear of our own death or to a myriad of other emotions.[4] The point to remember is that grief is a natural response to death, and liturgy can be a valuable means of working with that grief.

Viewed from a psychological perspective, the funeral and its accompanying rituals provide an opportunity for acting out and working through some painful but deeply significant feelings, of coming to terms with a new identity. This suggests to me a number of practical pastoral observations concerning the way we pastors treat the crisis of death.

First, there is a need to claim and affirm a grieving person's feelings as valid responses to death. Grief is not a sign of emotional instability or spiritual weakness. Grief is evidence of the sundering of love, attachment, and relationship by death. Jesus wept over his beloved Jerusalem and its coming destruction, and he wept at the death of his friend Lazarus. "See how he loved him," the bystanders rightly observed when they saw him weep for Lazarus. In a time when many speak of death as "natural" and when an absence of any show of grief is said to be evidence of "strong faith" and when the normative ritual for death is said to be the "joyous funeral," we need to be reminded that grief is a natural, Christian response to the pain of death. We Christians do not "grieve *as others who have no hope*" (I Thess. 4:13 RSV; emphasis added), but we still grieve.[5] As Emily Dickinson said, "Parting is all we know of heaven and all we need to know of hell."

This suggests to me that we must guard against intellectualizations in our dealing with the bereaved. Grief is an emotional crisis. Easy answers and pious clichés can be used to suppress important feelings. ("No need to weep, he is with Jesus now.") Any attempt to help grieving persons by helping them deny the reality of death or repress their true feelings is not helpful. The emotional crisis of grief will show itself in physiological ways (sweating, tremors, illness). Therefore, movement such as walking, working, and ritual activities (processing into the church behind the body, helping to carry the coffin, kneeling for prayer, standing to sing, helping to cover the grave with dirt) can all be helpful in engaging grieving persons in acting out and working through their feelings. The abundance of words, concepts, and abstractions in too many funeral services and the paucity of symbols, actions, and movement are aspects of our liturgical response to death that should be changed.

Whenever the funeral becomes an encouragement to suppress feelings or to deny reality, the funeral becomes a detriment rather than an aid in the grief process. Feelings, even feelings that the person views as negative feelings, that can be acted out and expressed at the beginning, can eventually be integrated into a positive recovery. Suppressed pain or anger or fear has a way of surfacing later in more destructive ways (withdrawal, suicide, psychosomatic illnesses).

There is no way of escaping the pain of loss. It can be masked by drugs or alcohol or by pretending it doesn't exist, but sooner or later we must face the pain, let ourselves experience the full intensity of grief and come to terms with it. Trying to avoid the pain only delays and extends it, and unresolved grief is an extremely destructive force.[6]

The crisis of death must be overcome, but it must not be overcome prematurely. Talk of resurrection and Christian hope must not come before honest admission of the reality of death and grief. The liturgical events of Holy Week always affirmed that one must understand the bleakness of Good Friday before one can fully experience Easter joy. Could part of the current emphasis on joyful funerals or small, deemphasized private memorial services be just another attempt on our part to avoid and deny the reality of death? The

Catholic who was accustomed to the requiem Mass with its black vestments and mournful chants may wonder when he participates in the new Mass of the resurrection if there is any place for tears or for the anguish of grief amidst white vestments and Easter songs.[7]

These sociological and psychological observations about the functions of our liturgical response to the crisis of death suggest to me that pastors need to exercise care in their leadership of the church's worship in times of life crisis. I have read dozens of articles on grief in such journals as *Pastoral Psychology* and *The Journal of Pastoral Care,* and few even mention the funeral as a resource in working through the grief process—a commentary on our obsession with the one-to-one, psychologically-oriented style of pastoral care and our general insensitivity to the importance of the historic resources of the church in meeting human need.[8] On the other hand, many new funeral liturgies show a giddy, superficial joyfulness that shows ignorance of the pastoral function of the funeral and of its historic foundations.

Every funeral should be an occasion for the public acceptance of people's feelings at the time of the crisis of death. Feelings should be expressed and admitted rather than manipulated or proscribed. The pastor can be the key in encouraging honest confrontation with death. I vividly remember two pastors' different funeral sermons on the occasion of the death of two teen-agers who died in much the same way. Both teen-aged boys were killed in highway accidents. One pastor, seeking, no doubt, to speak a word of comfort to the family, said in the opening line of his sermon: "Do not grieve for Tom. He is not in that coffin; he is with Jesus." There is questionable theology and psychology in that statement. The other pastor, faced with a similar tragic death, opened his sermon with, "I do not understand why tragedies like this one happen. I will not try to explain it

109

away, and I will not tell you this is the way God wanted this boy's life to end." He then went on to speak of hope that goes beyond the tragedies and mysteries of this life. I think the second pastor came closer to affirming the family's feelings at that moment and speaking to those feelings rather than dismissing or denying them. He also came closer to an authentic Christian theology of life and death.

As in any act of worship, actions are often more important than words. Protestant worship tends to be congregationally passive and pastorally verbose. This is particularly true of our funerals. We need to recover the symbolic richness of many of our older funeral practices. The preparation of the body, the building of the casket, the arrangements for the funeral, were once done by family and friends. We have increasingly given over these acts to paid professionals. Pastors and congregations need to assert themselves more in the planning and directing of funerals. Too many funeral services are done in impersonal, architecturally and symbolically nondescript funeral chapels. Too many funeral services are brief presentations by the pastor for the family rather than participatory, congregational experiences of Christian worship. The use of a creed or affirmation of faith, congregational hymn (rather than the all-too-frequent tear-jerking funeral solo), responsive readings, and congregational prayers can be means of involving family and friends in true worship. The use of a pall can be a way of avoiding the ostentation that often accompanies our funerals. Even seemingly insignificant acts such as the tossing of bits of dirt upon the coffin at the cemetery can be helpful ways of acting out and working through grief through symbolic acts.

I think funerals should be personalized to some extent. While the extended eulogy is usually out of place at a Christian funeral, it is crucial that we recognize that we are responding not to death in general but to the death of a specific person. The person's Christian name, by which that person was baptized, married, and buried, should be mentioned. But long dissertations on the alleged virtues of the deceased are inappropriate at a Christian funeral because of our belief in the equality of death and our recognition that, at time of death, we hope not in our own virtues or deeds but, "Our hope is in the name of the Lord."

Those of us who affirm the tradition of Word and sacrament should also be sensitive to the importance of scripture and sermon as an opportunity for the pastor to voice some important Christian affirmations in the face of death as well as to teach and interpret the mystery of our finitude and our Christian hope. Sacramentally, the relationship of death to baptism might be reflected upon. Death is also a historically and theologically appropriate occasion for the celebration of the Lord's Supper. Remembrance of our baptism when death occurs is a reminder of our continuing dependence on God's love in birth and death and of our lifelong relationship to divine grace. The celebration of the Lord's Supper is a reminder of the death of Jesus as a precursor of our death and of the resurrection of Christ. It points the way toward the communion of saints and the heavenly banquet in the kingdom of God. In a death-denying culture where death is looked upon as a bizarre intrusion and the resurrection is regarded as a naïve fantasy, a pastor might see every funeral as a time for proclaiming, with evangelistic and missionary zeal, the radically honest and hopeful Christian word at the time of death among modern people who are infatuated with youth and who delude themselves into thinking that we have a natural right to immortality on our own terms.

In his autobiography *Once to Every Man and Nation*, William Sloane Coffin, Jr., records his response to a friend's funeral, which demonstrates how the liturgy of the funeral, when combined with the needs of people, can serve as an act of evangelism and a call to faith:

In my senior year a good friend was killed in an automobile accident. Sitting in Dwight Chapel waiting for the funeral service to begin, I was filled with angry thoughts. My friend's death seemed to be one more bit of evidence to prove the fatuousness of believing in an all-powerful, all-loving God when, as any sensitive person could see, the entire surface of the earth was soaked with the tears and the blood of the innocent. Maliciously I had noted outside that the priest had a typically soft face over his hard collar. Now as he started down the aisle toward the altar he began to intone unctuously Job's famous words: "The Lord gave and the Lord hath taken away; blessed be the name of the Lord." From the aisle seat where I was sitting I could have stuck out my foot and tripped him up, and might easily have done so, had my attention not been arrested by a still, small voice, as it were, asking, "Coffin, what part of that sentence are you objecting to?" Naturally I thought it was the second part, "The Lord hath taken away," spoken all too facilely by the priest. But suddenly I realized it was the first. Suddenly I caught the full impact of "The Lord *gave*": the world very simply is not ours, at best we're guests. It was not an understanding I relished nor one, certainly, to clear up all my objections to my friend's death. But as I sat quietly now at his funeral, I realized that it was probably the understanding against which all the spears of human pride had to be hurled and shattered. Then, thank God, the organist played Bach's great chorale prelude, "Christus Stand in Todes Band." It was genuinely comforting. And it made me think that religious truths, like those of music, were probably apprehended on a deeper level than they were ever comprehended. . . . So the leap of faith was really a leap of action. Faith was not believing without proof; it was trusting without reservation. While such insights were hardly enough to convert me, the experience set me to wondering all over again.[9]

Many congregations will need to be reeducated or made more conscious of the value of our funerals and their related rituals. Unfortunately, we have been teaching them wrong things by the way we have done many funerals in the past. Obviously, when a family is in the throes of grief, that may not be the most opportune time to change their ideas about funerals. Pastoral care needs to be exercised before that time. Sermons and discussion groups on death, grief, and funerals may be helpful in getting people to think about matters they may not want to think about. Well-planned and well-led funerals will be the best way to teach what the Christian funeral should be.

Some churches urge their members to fill out a funeral questionnaire in which each adult member has an opportunity to think about and specify wishes for his or her funeral. Pastors who have used these forms report that they provide an excellent opportunity for some significant pastoral conversations with parishioners about their feelings about death and related matters. It is also an expression of pastoral accessibility and openness to discuss death now or in the future. The funeral questionnaire is then filed at the church for future reference. Such questionnaires can be a kind way to help one's family make decisions when one dies and avoid costly or unnecessary funeral practices if a family is confident that "he wanted it this way." Some carefully worked out, congregationally approved statement about procedures and purposes of funerals at a church can also be helpful in preparing people for death and grief and guiding them in the planning of a funeral.[10]

The Purpose of the Christian Funeral

All of which raises what is perhaps the most basic question regarding funerals. When I ask people, "What is the purpose of the Christian funeral?" they often respond with something like: "A funeral is for the living. It is mainly of help to the grieving family." While I hope it is clear from the above discussion that the funeral does help meet the acute needs of those who are currently going through the crisis of grief, the limitation of a funeral's function to an act of pastoral care for the living shows a lack of appreciation for the communal, social function of the funeral and a possible confusion about the purpose of Christian worship and the nature of Christian pastoral care.

A funeral is not only a therapeutic experience for the grieving family. It is also an opportunity for others within the congregation to prepare for their own future grief situations. The person who has never attended a funeral until he experiences acute grief is at a great disadvantage in not knowing how people are to act, think, and feel at the time of grief. To remind us again, liturgy is education. The funeral liturgy is a vitally necessary part of our preparation for death and bereavement before they occur. Every person's funeral, whether the person was close to us or not, provides an occasion for all of us to think about a life crisis that, without our participation in the funeral, we might not think about at all.

Related to this communal and educative function of the funeral is yet another function of a funeral. A funeral gives people the opportunity to deal with their own unfinished grief from prior bereavements. We find that we are especially empathetic with someone whose child has died if our child has died. We grieve with them, in great part, because we are continuing to grieve for ourselves. The pain of bereavement is probably never fully healed in a person. By putting us back in touch with continuing inner pain that we may have suppressed or denied, the funeral provides a manageable, ritualized way to continue our grief work.

This is a major reason why the trend toward private ceremonies and small family services may be bad for pastoral care and worship in the church. Such closed, small-group settings lose the whole meaning of the funeral as a communal acting-out process. To deny community participation in the grief process is to cut off grieving persons from the major resource for dealing with their grief. A funeral may be primarily for the grieving family, but it is not exclusively for them. It is for all of us. *A funeral, like every other act of Christian worship, is for the church!* True Christian worship is never a private matter. Every service of worship, judged by the criteria for full Christian worship, should be a communal, participatory event. Positive pastoral values are lost when any worship service—wedding, funeral, baptism, or Eucharist—becomes a private, noncommunal affair.

To define a funeral as being "for the living" or "for the family" raises theological questions. As we noted in an earlier chapter, Protestant worship has too often degenerated into emotional manipulation of people because the people are often thought to be the reason for and the central focus of worship. If a funeral is for the family or if a wedding is for the bride and groom, then whatever the family or the bride and groom want should be the basis of the service. The family's wishes become the only values that guide the service. If the service is for the family, then what makes it a specifically Christian service, and what makes it a service of *worship?*

Against the definition of the purpose of a funeral as being "for the family," I argue that the purpose is the same for a funeral as for any service of Christian worship: to worship God. The primary reason for our congregating to worship is not to focus upon ourselves and our desires but to focus upon God and God's relationship to us. The centrality of the funeral within the grief process, at least for the church, is not that a funeral is a good therapeutic aid to psychological well-being (which it often is) but that a funeral is an excellent time to focus upon God and our life and death in the light of God's love for us in Jesus Christ. It is pastorally unwise and theologically questionable to let the dead person's life, no matter how saintly that life may have been, become the center of attention at a funeral because, finally, the most relevant thing at the time of death is the never-ending grace and love of God. This is not to say that our funerals need to become more theological and less pastoral. Rather it is to say that as our funerals become more explicitly and intentionally theological they will become more pastorally helpful. For finally, I think, we Christians must affirm that grief and the pain of loss are best assuaged, not by romantic talk by Kübler-Ross about the "natural" quality of death or by nonbiblical speculations on our claim of the eternality of the soul, but rather by our bold affirmation of the nature of God.[11] In other words, we hope, not on the basis of who we are but on the basis of who God is. This does not deny, as I suggested above, that some part of the funeral needs to be specific and recognize that a particular person whom we have known and loved has died, nor does it deny that the grieving family may have specific requests or needs that will need to be focused upon in the service. It merely reminds us that the basic, primary purpose and focus of the funeral is theological, thereby enabling us to be more significantly pastoral.

How helpful it is to a grieving family, shocked, bereft, and speechless, to be brought into a funeral that is a true service of worship and to be encouraged to rise to their feet and join the congregation in singing something strong like "A Mighty Fortress Is Our God" or "Immortal, Invisible, God Only Wise." As a pastor I have been deeply moved by seeing a grieving family rise to their feet during the affirmation of faith and, with tears streaming down their faces, not believing yet believing, not understanding yet hoping, joining with their fellow Christians in saying, "I believe in God the Father Almighty, Creator of heaven and earth." Or ponder the pastoral significance of the use of some of the great psalms within the funeral service, so penetrating in their honest confession of frustration and loss ("My God, my God, why have you forsaken me?") and yet also encouraging in their honest vision of hope. The quiet, firm sureness of the pastor in leading a funeral service, combined with pastoral openness and acceptance of a family's feelings of grief, will say much to the grieving family and the congregation as a whole about Christian response to death. Giddy, Pollyanna, pasted-on smiles and back-slapping assurances are as theologically and pastorally out of place as cold, bleak, impersonal morbidity. My contention is that carefully planned, theologically full, and well-led funeral liturgies will do much in helping us to help the grieving people and the congregation as a whole in the time of the life crisis of death and bereavement.

A Funeral Sermon

The following episode is taken from a letter one of my former students wrote me soon after he graduated from seminary and became pastor of two small United Methodist churches in a rural area of South Carolina.

Setting: (Here is the pastor's own explanation of the case situation.) "Sunday afternoon one of my members called to ask if I would do a funeral for a relative who had just died. I had seen the man twice in the hospital, once just before he died on Saturday. This man was about seventy and had not been to church since he was about four years old. He did not even go into the church for his parents' funerals. He was not a member of any church, and the family did not have a minister; so they called me Sunday afternoon to do the funeral at the funeral home the next day. I agreed to do it since I had seen him (I had talked frankly with him and with his family about his struggles with the church) and because I thought it gave me a chance to do some evangelizing (I have enclosed the sermon for your impressions)"

Sermon: Facing the prospect of death is a difficult enough task, but trying to face death thinking you are somehow separated from the love of God is almost unbearable. Yet in the last few days before his death, that was the task Henry Smith faced. I know that is the case because I talked to him on Saturday afternoon, and he told me that he realized some of the mistakes he had made throughout his life. The one he regretted most and that bothered him most was that he had not been to church in many years. He had been good to many people throughout his life and had many friends, but he knew on Saturday afternoon that he had missed the church. He was facing his last days feeling that he was somehow separated from the love of God. Facing death without the support of the church and feeling separated from the love of God is a lonely experience that I tried to help Mr. Smith think through.

We read in scripture that if God is for us, who is against us? Who shall separate us from the love of Christ? For I am sure that neither death nor life, nor angels nor principalities nor things present nor things to come nor powers nor height nor depth nor anything else in creation will be able to separate us from the love of God in Christ Jesus our Lord. I tried to tell Mr. Smith that our God still does care, that he is for us not against us. I told him that the church was still interested in him. That is why I was there. I told him that it was never too late to ask God to be with him, that in fact He was with him. Before I left we prayed together. In our prayer we thanked God for his life; we asked God's forgiveness for those things that, if he had the chance he would do differently; we asked for love and peace and courage.

118

Yes, on Saturday he missed the church and felt lonely. He felt separated from the love of God and was afraid, but I told him the church was behind him and cared for him, which gave him strength, and that God was with him and loved him, which gave him hope. I think Henry felt the love of a God who had loved Henry all his life with only one desire—to love him (as he does now) *forever*. That is the kind of God we have. Who shall separate us from the love of Christ? No one. I believe Henry Smith understood that and believed and was comforted by it Saturday afternoon, and therefore he was able to die in courage and hope. Let us praise God!

Reflection: Here was a young minister caught in a situation many pastors have been through: leading a funeral for a person who has had no relationship with the church. What should one do in such cases? If a funeral is mainly an occasion to celebrate the achievements of the deceased, then the pastor has a real problem. In the interest of simple honesty, the pastor may be tempted to simply admit that the church is at a disadvantage in such cases, say as little as possible about the person, and let the liturgy speak for itself. Or, in the interest of pastoral concern for the family, the pastor may be tempted to say too much, attempting to soothe over the family's sorrow and the congregation's questions with talk about the basic goodness of the person regardless of his lack of religious commitment.

But if the funeral is primarily a service of worship, a time to celebrate our faith in the context of this person's life and death, then the pastoral problem on an occasion such as this is quite different. The problem and the opportunity for the pastor in that case will be how to be honest about our questions, pain, and grief and yet be faithful to the gospel— which is probably where we are at *every* funeral. This

119

is where I see the struggle for this pastor. He is honest about Mr. Smith's situation. No doubt the pastor's honesty in facing Mr. Smith's life and feelings at the time of death was an aid to the family in facing their own feelings about his death. If the pastor had avoided mention of it, he would have conveyed to the family the feeling that Mr. Smith's lack of church commitment was an unmentionable sin. The pastor has faced it squarely, thus encouraging the family to do the same.

There is a question here of respecting pastoral confidences. However, if it is true that there was frank and open discussion of Henry's struggle with the church, then the pastor's open discussion of that struggle may have been justified in the sermon. Also, one gets the uncomfortable feeling that the pastor may have been tempted here to say too much, focusing too exclusively upon Henry and his struggles: "I believe that Henry Smith understood it and believed." There is also some question as to whether the pastor's own description of his handling of the situation ("I told him the church—") may have slipped into clerical self-justification. If the sermon were heard by the congregation in either of these ways, then Henry or the pastor may have gotten in the way of the proclamation of God.

But by focusing on scripture (Romans 8), the pastor effectively placed a current situation alongside the Christian tradition so that the tradition could illuminate the situation. He also claimed and affirmed his visit with Mr. Smith at the hospital as the presence of the church. Mr. Smith did not really die *ex ecclesia*. The pastor, the church's representative, was there with him. So was the church's scripture. Mr. Smith's hope is the same as every person's hope in death: our hope is in God. I am reminded of the way the liturgy used to handle such occasions. There is a prayer in the old *Book of Common Prayer* that was used for the funeral of a person who was not a communicating member of a church. It refers to Jesus' statement about having sheep who are not members of this fold but are still his sheep! I am continually impressed by how often the older liturgies were able to deal theologically and pastorally with such matters in relatively effective ways. Those of us who share the free-church tradition often find ourselves having to deal with difficult pastoral situations by creating our own liturgical response *ex nihilo* (as I think this young pastor was attempting to do in this sermon). The lack of formal liturgical resources is both an opportunity and a burden for free-church pastors, requiring them to exercise even more care and pastoral wisdom in their leadership on such occasions than do their counterparts in the "liturgical" churches.

The sermon ends on an affirmative, strong note. In the end, I think that it is a sermon, not a eulogy. "That is the kind of God we have. . . . Let us praise God!" I hear education, proclamation, edification, and inter-pretation at work here. The pastor was correct in calling this an act of evangelism. Of course, the sermon needs to be placed within the context of the total liturgy and all the pastoral and liturgical acts associated with pastoral leadership at this time of crisis. One should note in this regard that the pastor was able to preach a warm, confessional, appropriate sermon, in great part because a great amount of pastoral care and work had gone on *before* the funeral. Without those two prior hospital visits, the sermon could not have been preached in this way, which underscores the integral relationship between day-to-day pastoral care and leadership of the liturgy during the life crisis of death.

121

VI
Liturgy and Learning: The Wedding

In the last chapter we focused on the funeral as a ritualized means of helping us to cope with life's crises. We noted how any significant transition in life involves the movement across certain boundaries as we move from one identity or state of being to another. This movement across boundaries precipitates a crisis within the individual and within persons who are related to that individual. The church has always used a complex series of formal and informal rituals and liturgical acts to guide us through life's most difficult transitions.

In this chapter we will focus on the wedding service, the Service of Holy Matrimony, as an example of how we care for persons who make the difficult transition from singlehood to marriage. While our discussion of the funeral centered upon the funeral as a therapeutic and supportive way of coping with death and grief, this chapter will primarily focus upon the wedding as a ritualized means of educating people for a new life status.

Liturgy *is* education. The question before us in this chapter is not *whether* our people will learn when they worship. The question is, *What* will they learn when we lead them in worship? We sometimes forget that we are engaged in education every time we lead the congregation in prayer or in the Lord's Supper or in any other occasion of public worship. Unfortunately, people often learn things when they worship that we may not have intended to teach them—but they still learn.

When a couple bring their baby to the pastor to be "done" and the pastor agrees to baptize the child in spite of the lack of parental understanding or commitment to the faith and the church, the parents have learned something about baptism. When a young couple are married by a pastor in a service of their own devising which is heavy on poetry by Rod McKuen and Kahlil Gibran and light on Christian theology, the couple have learned something about marriage. Once again, the question is not *whether* we teach within the liturgy; the question is whether what we teach is *Christian* or not!

I agree with my colleague at Duke, John Westerhoff, who reminds us that the liturgy is always an occasion for learning, and at the same time the liturgy is always in need of the reflection and refinement that should occur within the catechetical program of the church:

Liturgy and learning have been linked since the birth of the Christian era, but of late they have become estranged. . . . Religious educators and liturgists have gone their separate ways and attempts to reunite their various concerns have tended to confuse the issue and distort important distinctions between them. Some religious educators have made the serious mistake of speaking of teaching *by* or *with* the liturgy, thereby reducing the liturgy to a didactic act. To *use* the liturgy is to do it violence. Of course, we learn through the liturgy. . . . Our rituals shape and form us in fundamental ways. But our liturgies properly should be understood as ends and not as means. . . . Both liturgy and catechesis are pastoral activities through which divine revelation is made known, mature faith is enhanced and enlivened, and persons are prepared and stimulated for their vocation in the world. . . .

Liturgy is the actions and catechesis the reflections of the community of faith. . . . Liturgy nurtures the community of faith through celebrative symbolic acts of faith. Catechesis nurtures the community of faith through mindful attempts to communicate and reflect upon the story (myth) which underlies and informs these acts of faith.[1]

Our discussion of the funeral noted the three stages of what anthropologists call rites of passage: separation, transition, and reincorporation.[2] As with the funeral, if a wedding were to be analyzed as a rite of passage, we could detect a complex series of stated and unstated ritual acts that move two persons from being regarded as individuated singles into a unified couple.

But in this chapter we shall be most interested in how a wedding, as a rite of passage and as a liturgical event of the church, functions as an educational activity for the church. The question might then be asked, What do education and learning have to do with the task of pastoral care? Education and pastoral care have nothing in common if pastoral care is conceived of only in terms of psychological support, in the administration of certain therapeutic techniques aimed at the maintenance or reestablishment of personal emotional equilibrium, and so forth. But if *pastoral care* encompasses the wide range of pastoral acts aimed at the healing, guiding, sustaining, and reconciling of persons within the Body of Christ and the complex ways in which pastors care for and upbuild that body, then surely education can be one aspect of pastoral care.

While we have been right, in the past few years, to see the limitations of purely cognitive, inductive, educationally-oriented approaches to our human problems, we must overcome the notion that the support and guidance of persons require only deductive pastoral acts in which the community and its pastoral representatives take care not to intrude upon a person's own individual values or lack of values. We must again affirm

124

that people can be healed, supported, and cared for by helping them clarify their values and concepts, by putting forward a conceptual framework upon which they are able to make meaning of their often disordered world, by telling them the Story in terms that can be heard and affirmed as *their* story, by proclaiming the faith in such a way as it becomes *their* faith.

Pastoral Problems with Weddings

The Service of Holy Matrimony is a relative latecomer to our worship services. In its earliest years, the church let civil authorities oversee the marriage of a man and a woman and then gave its public blessing to the marriage during a Sunday worship service. Gradually, the rite of marriage moved from the civil court to the front porch of the church into the church itself, where it became a distinct service of worship in the late Middle Ages. As with many other liturgical acts, the church simply adopted many pagan customs regarding rites of marriage and put them in a Christian context. Quaint customs like the bride's feeding the groom the wedding cake, the carrying of the bride over the threshold, and the exchange of rings, all relate to earlier pagan customs. The present form of the service itself and much of the language like "to have and to hold" and "till death us do part" are legal terms that relate to property rights and legal contracts between two people and reflect the jurisprudential origins of the service.[3]

While nearly every rite within the Christian liturgy contains acts and language that harken back to pagan antecedents, the Service of Holy Matrimony is replete with former pagan practices. It thus represents a curious amalgam of the sacred and the profane, the civil and the religious, and, at most any wedding, the sublime and the ridiculous. This has probably led many pastors to wonder if the church would have been better off to have left the service of marriage outside the church!

Which leads me to an opening psychological observation about us pastors and our leadership of weddings. I have noted widespread ministerial uneasiness with the marriage service. Invariably, pastors report that the leading of the Service of Holy Matrimony causes them as much anxiety, frustration, and anger as any other service of worship. They will complain that they are disgusted with the "pagan display" of many weddings, the crude material extravagance, and the fact that many a bride and groom have no idea what a Christian wedding is. They will tell you that if couples were more honest, many would confess that they are simply "going through with it to please our parents." Many pastors labor heroically to ensure that the music will be appropriately "religious" and that the couple, their families, and friends are suitably "serious" about the whole matter.

While I fully sympathize with the dismay of pastors who ask a couple why they want a church wedding only to be told something like, "She wants a big, beautiful service with lots of flowers"; while I fully support the efforts of pastors to make each wedding a full service of Christian worship; I wonder if some of our pastoral uneasiness with the wedding may say as much about the inadequacies of our own theology as it says about our manifest desire for liturgical purity. I wonder if some of our pastoral resistance to the weddings in which we are called to officiate is rooted in our own personal limitations.

The fact is, a wedding is much more than a limited spiritual, or solemn, and holy event as we usually define these words. A wedding is the liturgical ritualized celebration of the sexual union of two persons. Amidst all the flowers, white lace, and soft ethereal music, we sometimes obscure the fact that a few hours later, this couple will be in bed together. In fact, that may be part of the attraction of the flowers and the lace. They obscure the essential, "earthy," corporeal, human event that is taking place amidst this "heavenly" setting. We are dealing here with sex, sexual union, procreation, male and female, and all the deep, sometimes threatening, always mysterious power that these realities hold within themselves.

And that, I suspect, is one reason I and my fellow pastors have often been a bit squeamish about the Service of Holy Matrimony. We may affirm our belief in the Incarnation, our agreement that sex is a gift from God, that divine love may be revealed within human beings and earthly activities. But the service of marriage requires us to not only affirm these beliefs intellectually but to openly claim them, symbolize them, act them out in a public declaration that the sexual union of a man and a woman is full of eternal significance. Every time the church celebrates a marriage, it is arguing, against all our Manichaean and Docetic tendencies, that marriage is "an honorable estate, instituted of God."

Witness our belabored attempts to make weddings "serious" and "religious" as if we were dealing with a rather questionable human activity that somehow needs to be whitewashed and purified before it can be brought into the church. Liturgiologists speak of the wedding as a latecomer to our Christian liturgical life and as being in grave need of purging of its "pagan" elements. There is also much stress, in my opinion, too much stress, upon the necessity and the potential effectiveness of premarital counseling to ensure that a couple know what they are doing and are "suitably prepared" for marriage. I have heard pastors brag that they require four or five hours of such premarital counseling which includes the administration of standardized personality tests, financial advice, and physiological instruction. All this in spite of many researchers' belief that such before-the-event, forced counseling (indoctrination?) is of little significant or lasting consequence for the couple.[4] The stress on premarital counseling suggests three things to me: (1) It is a commentary on how little faith we have in the historic, public, liturgical acts the church has traditionally used to counsel, educate, and support marrying couples (the wedding) and how much faith we have in one-to-one counseling techniques. (2) The counseling may be just another clerical effort to "clean up" the wedding of its all-too-human symbolic, acted-out quality and make marriage a safe, cognitively, and/or psychologically structured event. (3) We doubt that it is possible for God to join anyone together (as the service explicitly claims) without our human manipulation of the bond.

In so doing we are not only revealing our own clerical distrust of the body and human sexuality, but we are also *teaching* the couple who is to marry and the witnessing congregation that marriage must somehow be purified, legitimatized, sanctified, understood, and rationalized before it is "holy." Nothing could be further from the biblical testimony on human sexuality in marriage or the church's theology of matrimony as revealed in the service of marriage itself.[5] The purpose of the Service of Holy Matrimony is not to put some sugar coating on an essentially distasteful human necessity. It is not to sanctify and make holy what would otherwise be fleshly and immoral without our liturgical formulas. Nor is it to rationally elucidate the mystery of sexual union (which, contrary to Masters and Johnson, cannot be done). The purpose of the service is to claim the union of this man and woman as an act of a loving God, as representative of God's ultimate purpose in all creation, and as a joyous sign of God's continuing love and creativity in our midst. It is a blessing of the process of union.

For some time now it has been fashionable for many couples to write their own wedding ceremony. I have let couples design their own weddings, but I have rarely been pleased with the results. In general, two things bother me about this practice. First, the services are invariably theologically inadequate to say nothing of poetically prosaic and liturgically insipid. The services are often full of high-sounding talk about love and happiness and joy and are empty of solid biblical content or solid, concrete affirmations of faith. Couples who began by saying that they objected to the archaic language of the older service ended up with a new service that sounded more like a sorority initiation ceremony than a prelude to a life together. The service said much about love, joy, and happiness and little about fidelity, endurance, and commitment.

Second, if a wedding is a rite of passage in the sense of being the Christian community's effort to help a man and a woman move from singlehood to marriage through the use of certain ritualized acts that support, guide, and educate, then is there any pastoral justification for letting the recipients of this liturgical act of pastoral care determine the content, form, and nature of that care? This may sound like a retreat from my earlier observations of the possibly negative aspects of our liturgical fastidiousness concerning weddings. But I in no way wish to support the pastoral irresponsibility that occurs when a pastor says, in effect, "Oh, well, it's *their* wedding, and they have a right to say what it should be like." It is their wedding in the sense that their love and their vows have occasioned this gathering. As in our discussion of funerals, we must note that we do have two specific, distinct persons here, not merely a bride and groom in an abstract sense. They will have specific needs, requests, unique expressions of who they are and what they want to be, and the pastor may wish to explore ways in which these specifics can be expressed and informed through the worship service. But, as with the funeral, the wedding is a service of *worship*. There is nothing "private" about this moment. Like the funeral, the wedding belongs to the whole church. Its intent is to do and say more than to merely express the whims and idiosyncracies of any individual couple (or of any individual couple's parents, for that matter). The minister, at the very beginning of the service, proclaims that we are gathered "before God and these witnesses," thus affirming the public, corporate nature of the wedding.

Recently I attended a wedding for which the couple had written their own ritual. The minister greeted the congregation with these words: "We are here to celebrate the love of John and Susan." If that were the reason for our gathering, then, whatever we were doing, we were not gathering for *worship*! As we said in the beginning of this book, worship has first to do with God. It would have been more helpful for the minister to begin with, "We are here to celebrate the love and work of God who has brought John and Susan together and without whom there is no true or lasting union." Note that the old wedding service begins, not with comments on the alleged virtues of the bride and groom, but with talk about God who "instituted" this "honorable estate" that Christ "adorned and beautified with his presence in Cana of Galilee." Then comes the "therefore" which is addressed not only to the bride and groom but to *everyone* in the congregation: "It is therefore not to be entered into unadvisedly, but reverently, discreetly."

The point is not to be liturgical purists or theological dilettantes; the point is that, like other liturgical acts, the wedding will only be of lasting, decisive pastoral consequence as it is an act of worship, a Christian rite of passage that takes seriously the difficulty of this life transition and the need for careful education, proclamation, affirmation, confession, forgiveness, offering, and all the other pastoral and priestly functions of any true service of worship.

The most basic objection I have to most of the wedding services I have seen couples construct is not that they have violated church law or principles of good taste but that they have cheated themselves of some of the important meanings this act of worship could have for them. They have merely given us a summary of where their thoughts and values are at this particular moment in their lives in regard to marriage and have received virtually no prodding, guiding, counseling, or teaching from the church. One response from the church to the request by a couple to write their own wedding might be (and I am speaking tongue in cheek): "Who are you to be writing your marriage? We have been about this business of bringing men and women together for a very long time, and we need to say some things to you, see you do certain things, help you to affirm and let go of certain things; and this is all too important to entrust to any one couple in any one generation." We need, in other words, to show the couple that this act of marriage is too difficult, too risky, too demanding, to neglect the full range of the church's resources at this time in life. Much pastoral care is needed at the moment of marriage, and our principal way of showing that care is through the Service of Holy Matrimony and its complex of rituals.

All of which should now enable us to look at this service of worship with greater sensitivity to its importance—particularly its educational importance. We are defining *educational* here in the broad sense as "the deliberate, systematic, and sustained effort to transmit or evoke knowledge, attitudes, values, skills, and sensibilities."[6] This definition limits our observation of the wedding as an educational act to those parts of the wedding ritual that have an intentional, systematic, long-term quality. As we noted earlier, people often learn things from us that we did not intend to teach. But we are concerned here with those ways in which the marriage service represents an act by which the church cares for people who are in the transition to married life, those systematic and ritualized means by which the church attempts to transmit or evoke the values, perspectives, and knowledge the Christian community has deemed necessary for a Christian marriage. We will also be limiting our observations to the wedding service itself. This is not to deny the appropriateness and even the necessity of a wide range of other "deliberate, systematic, and sustained" efforts on the part of the church to educate a couple for marriage. Nor is this meant to *use* the liturgy for didactic activity for the people which destroys its central focus of praise and response to God. It is simply to focus on an often overlooked resource for fulfilling the educational duty of the church at the time of marriage—the rite of Holy Matrimony itself.

The Service[7]

Nearly every liturgy for matrimony begins with a rubric, addressed to the minister,

the minister is enjoined diligently to instruct those requesting his offices for their prospective marriage in the Christian significance of the holy estate into which they seek to enter.

While we noted, above, the limitations of premarital counseling, this is not to deny the necessity for intentional, careful, pastoral, and educational activities before the wedding. It may be helpful for the pastor to envision premarital counseling sessions as occasions to prepare a couple to participate more fully in the wedding liturgy itself. This might take the form of first having the couple ask questions about the ritual, then having the pastor go through the entire service, step-by-step, interpreting to the couple what the church is trying to say and show in this service. Then the pastor and the couple could discuss ways in which the service might be modified or adapted to the couple's own needs or desires. The very act of planning the wedding can be an educational event whereby the couple are enabled, through the pastor's guidance, to articulate and evaluate their own beliefs about marriage in light of the church's historic witness in regard to marriage.

Of course, there are couples who may have serious reservations about affirming some of the beliefs that are expressed in the Service of Holy Matrimony. The pastor should provide an atmosphere in premarital counseling sessions in which the couple's misgivings can be honestly expressed and sensitively explored. If a couple proposes a major change in the service, then it is the responsibility of the pastor, as the representative of the community of faith, to decide if their proposal is consistent with the community's beliefs. If the change is deemed inconsistent, then the pastor must either work with the couple to reach some mutually acceptable compromise, or the pastor may refuse to marry the couple.

This is not to say that the pastor approaches each couple with the attitude "Show me that you are worthy of Christian marriage and thoroughly orthodox in your beliefs." It is simply to affirm that the possibility of saying no must be there. If it is not, then we are forever in danger of being irresponsible and uncaring in our valueless dealings with a couple who may be in great need of responsible and caring support from the community and its reservoir of values.

We must also remind ourselves that a wedding, if it is a true service of worship, is always an occasion for edification, conversion, rebirth, proclamation, witness, and all the other evangelistic acts that may occur within

Christian worship. While we do not wish to delude the couple into thinking that they can publicly affirm anything regardless of their own sincerity or commitment, we do believe that the wedding itself can be an occasion for new insights, deepened commitments, and conversion. In one sense, we would be rather unrealistic if we were to demand that a couple "understand and believe what the church understands and believes about marriage" prior to their own marriage. Marriage may be one of those human-faith experiences that is fully understood only from the inside, from the actual, lifelong, continuing experience of marriage. Which is to remind us again of the communal, corporate nature of this (and every other) significant act of worship. A wedding is not only a learning opportunity for the couple who is marrying. It is also an opportunity for all the rest of us to renew our vows, to continue to penetrate and experience the full range of meanings within our own marital unions, and to instruct and invite those within the worshiping congregation who may enter into future marriage. The wedding is for all of us.

As we move into the words and actions of the service itself, this communal, educational function is immediately apparent. The first words spoken in the traditional service are addressed, not to the bride and groom, but to the congregation.

Dearly, beloved, we are gathered together here in the sight of God, and in the presence of these witnesses, to join together *this man and this woman* in holy matrimony.

The church then affirms that marriage is "an honorable estate," instituted by God from the time of creation (using the rather questionable proof text of Genesis 1 f.). We sometimes forget that there was a period in our history when marriage was considered less than honorable, a second-class arrangement for those

Christians who were unable to attain the ideal of celibacy. This Reformation service seeks to counter these doubts about matrimony, doubts that (as we indicated earlier) may still be with us today, even if in more subtle form.

Then we are reminded that marriage is "not to be entered into unadvisedly." The older *Book of Common Prayer* service once had here, "to satisfy men's carnal lusts and appetites like brute beasts, that have no understanding, but reverently, discreetly." I have often regretted that Victorian sensibilities removed these earthy, honest words from our service! At least then, no one could accuse the church of naïveté about the darker side of human nature or the results of unrestrained hedonism. Once again, I am forever impressed with the realism and frankness of some of our older liturgical forms, especially when compared to some of our so-called contemporary attempts at liturgical expression. Anyone who would deny our potential for fulfilling "carnal lusts and appetites" like "brute beasts" has not looked at the cinema section of the daily newspaper lately.

Even the now-humorous "If any man can show just cause why they may not lawfully be joined together," a vestige from the legal-contract origins of the service, can be seen as having contemporary significance as a public declaration that everyone present has a stake in this union and a responsibility to support it once it is made. Now is the time for frank disclosure of any serious impediments or else eternal "silence," free from malicious gossip, in support of the marriage.

Then the minister addresses the couple.

I require and charge you both, as you stand in the presence of God, before whom the secrets of all hearts are disclosed, that, having duly considered the holy covenant you are about to make, you do now declare before this company your pledge of faith, each to the other.

135

This highlights the central act of the service; the making of promises in the presence of God and the congregation. Then follows a somewhat regrettable statement of works righteousness.

Be well assured that if these solemn vows are kept inviolate, . . . God will bless your marriage, will grant you fulfillment in it, and will establish your home in peace.

Since God's gifts are unconditional, this statement is theologically questionable. Yet it can be seen as an attempt to remind the couple of the importance of their promises and their mutual responsibility in this union.

Then the church gets down to the nitty-gritty of the hard facts of life and the tough demands for life together. A declaration of intent is now required.

[Name], wilt thou have this woman to be thy wedded wife, to live together in the holy estate of matrimony? Wilt thou love her, comfort her, honor and keep her, in sickness and in health; and forsaking all other keep thee only unto her so long as ye both shall live?

It has always interested me that the church has never asked, "Do you love her?" The church asks, "*Will* you love her?" In our faith, love is not so much a feeling, for we have always (against some psychologists in our midst) judged feelings to be rather fickle and of limited help in establishing relationships. Against all pagan definitions of *love*, the church here defines *love* as an act of the will, something one can decide and promise to do. Compared to some of our culture's current usage of the word *love*, here is a rather radical redefinition of the word which demands a promise of fidelity even amidst the hard vicissitudes of life and a promise of exclusiveness even amidst all the other claims upon our love and affections.

I suspect that, at this point in the marriage service, the liturgy expands from pastoral and educational concerns to encompass missional, confessional, and evangelistic concerns. In a world of impermanence and infidelity, what more radical witness might the church have than to boldly proclaim this countercultural definition of *love* and its true conditions?[8]

Before the ritual moves through the separation phase of its rite of passage, separation occurs in the form of the traditional giving away of the bride by her parents. While this is a somewhat anachronistic holdover from the days when the woman was little more than parental property and is questionable in light of our current understandings of feminine equality, it is an attempt to show that marriage is not only a union of a man and a woman, it is also an alliance of two families. This act is also a symbol of the "two becoming one flesh." A new creation is occurring here. The parents must now give up their old claims; their child is now becoming another's mate. How many marriages have failed because the parents failed to understand this fact? Some of the new marriage services retain this symbolic act of giving and separation while changing its exclusivistic character by providing, at this point in the service, an opportunity for *both* sets of parents to pronounce their blessing upon the marriage. This act of blessing not only recognizes the needs and tensions that may be in the bride and groom in relationship to their parents, but it also acknowledges the needs and tensions within the parents at this significant (and sometimes painful) plateau in their own lives.

Then vows are exchanged. This is done both bodily and verbally. The service rubrics direct:

Then, the minister, receiving the hand of the woman from her father or other sponsor, shall cause the man with his right hand to take the woman by her right hand, and say after him . . .

This demonstrates the symbolic richness within the Service of Holy Matrimony. I have often observed, even in those churches that feel apathy or even disdain for sacramental, acted-out, symbolic acts within their worship; the service of marriage is invariably rich in processions, special dress, symbolic words and gestures, and a wide variety of sacramental actions, even if marriage itself is not defined as a sacrament.[9] In this case, the minister, representing the church, receives the bride's hand after she is separated from her parents, and then joins her to her mate. It is all very active, physical, and beautifully symbolic.

This physical acting out of the joining is followed by a verbal expression of the union. While it has been popular in recent years to encourage couples to memorize their vows and to repeat them from memory at this point, I personally prefer that couples repeat the words after the minister says them. While the former method does accentuate the vows as a personal expression of the couple's commitment, I think we must not lose sight of the fact that these vows are given by the Christian community as standards, requirements, and aids to the attainment of becoming "one flesh." This would seem to be better symbolized by repeating the vows after the minister speaks them. In any case the worship leader needs to be sensitive to the symbolic statements we implicitly make by the very manner in which we do them.

The vows themselves are indicative of what the community feels to be the requisites for a deep and enduring relationship between a man and a woman:

I, [Name], take thee, [Name], to be my wedded wife, to have and to hold, from this day forward, for better, for worse, for richer, for poorer, in sickness and in health, to love and to cherish, till death us do part, according to God's holy ordinance; and thereto I pledge thee my faith.

While the pledge of faithfulness is made in the presence of and with the guidance of the church, note that it is made *to* the other person. I have interpreted the "worse" here to mean that one pledges to endure even unhappiness, rather than to seek happiness apart from each other. We are saying here that happiness is not a suitable goal in itself. It is only a possible by-product of fidelity. Togetherness, union, completeness, are the primary virtues. There is also a kind of realism about life here. The two young people before the minister at the altar may not, in the bliss and potency of youth, adequately appreciate how love is tested in the trials of life. The church here affirms that love can only endure those trials through unconditional, lifelong fidelity "for better or worse." We once said that suffering could be ennobling. We once said that there were other, more important values to be followed in life than the achievement of personal happiness. Before we jetison these historic affirmations that are expressed here simply because they are currently unpopular and are continually difficult, we need to consider again their validity lest, in accommodating ourselves to the world, we forsake something the world may desperately need us to say—and say with boldness and confidence.

Then we have the giving and receiving of rings. A visible, physical act wherein, by the way, we Protestants state a traditional definition of a sacrament as "an outward and visible sign of an inward and spiritual grace" even though we have traditionally denied matrimony sacramental status.[10] (Speaking of bodily acts, the old *Book of Common Prayer* said, "With this ring I thee wed, *with my body I thee worship,* and with all my goods I thee endow, in the name of the Father, . . ." Even the most liberated sensualist might squirm under such language.)

Finally, the minister makes a public proclamation of the act that has just taken place,

Forasmuch as [Name] and [Name] have consented together in holy wedlock, and have witnessed the same before God and this company, and thereto have pledged their faith each to the other, . . . I pronounce that they are husband and wife together. . . . Those whom God hath joined together, let not man put asunder.

There is a final prayer by the pastor, the Lord's Prayer, and a benediction, or blessing, and the service is concluded on what should be a joyous and affirmative note.

In a day when many question whether it is humanly possible for a man and a woman to live together in mutuality and faithfulness for a moment much less a lifetime, when many glorify "do-your-own-thing" self-centeredness as liberation rather than risk union with another human being, when there are many in the church itself who would willingly accommodate the whims of secular culture rather than call people forth to courageous commitment,[11] the act of marriage itself has become an act of faith. Every time the church blesses the union of a couple in the Service of Holy Matrimony, it proclaims to them and to the world that love, fidelity, permanence, mutuality, self-giving, and receiving are possible—through God's grace. The fidelity these vows demand is not an obligation but an invitation to risk oneself in a relationship as free, as secure, as permanent, as challenging as God's relationship to us in Christ. Togetherness, union, creativity, are the fruits of the wedding of a man and woman, not unlike the fruits of the wedding of God with humanity in Christ. The church was right, in the opening lines of the marriage service, to see marriage as a human analogy for a divine-human experience, a human union "signifying unto us the mystical union which exists between Christ and his Church."

As was stated in the opening of this chapter, not only do Christian education and catechesis help prepare people to participate more meaningfully in the liturgy, part of the relationship between liturgy and education is also a continual reassessment on our part of what people are learning in our liturgy and how our liturgies can better express what the community wishes to proclaim in its acts of worship. No doubt, in reading over some of the affirmations the church has historically made in the Service of Holy Matrimony, it probably occurred to the reader that, whether due to our manner of leading this service or the archaic language or the nonliturgical accretions this service has acquired, the message of the service has often been lost.

In passing, I have a few suggestions for the pastor who wishes to make this service a more meaningful experience for the participants. First, it will help if we constantly remind ourselves that the wedding is a service of worship, judging it and planning it by the same norms and guidelines we apply to all worship services. This should immediately point up certain inadequacies in many of our weddings. If congregational participation, abundant use of scripture, preaching, the Eucharist, offering, confession, and forgiveness are considered to be necessary aspects of every worship service, then we should explore ways to make them a part of every service of marriage.[12] Where possible, weddings should be celebrated in the context of a regular Sunday worship service. Together, bride, groom, pastor, and congregation should search for new ways to better express our faith in Christian marriage. Postmarital counseling to which the pastor and the couple commit themselves, marriage-support and enrichment groups within the congregation, and preparation of youths and young adults for marriage through the church's catechetical program are among the ways we can prepare people to participate more meaningfully in the liturgy of the wedding and the "liturgy" they will move through each day of their marriage.

I hope this foregoing discussion indicates some of the theological and pastoral richness within the Service of

141

Holy Matrimony as well as its function as an educational act of the church. Perhaps, in an earlier age, the church could be somewhat nonchalant about how it prepared people to participate in this service and how this service was celebrated. Perhaps. But in our age, where sex has become an infatuation and a preoccupation, where love has been prostituted and emptied of much of its significance, where relationships in general between men and women have become problematic, and where marriage in particular has come under increasing attack, we must be quite intentional and careful in our leadership of the liturgy of matrimony. The learning that can occur therein can be crucial in the life and love of our people.

Whose Wedding?

A Pastoral Dialogue

The following dialogue occurred between the distinguished pastoral counselor and theologian Dr. Seward Hiltner and a parish minister.[13]

Pastor: Being in a university town until about a year ago we found that we were having more and more weddings in our church of young people who did not live in the community and who had not grown up in the parish. Invariably, the reason for making this kind of arrangement was the young man and the young woman did not want to go home and have a large social wedding with all the trappings. Living in a small community for all their lives they thought it was impossible, they couldn't do that to their parents, to go home and have a small wedding.

Hiltner: They probably wouldn't permit it.

Pastor: Yes. So they chose some sort of neutral ground on which to be married which I saw as a very positive kind of thing.

142

Hiltner: . . . I think you may be right. People really don't want a big shindig back home in the small town, so to speak. Of course, there's also the fact that their parents, but primarily the mama back there . . .

Pastor: Right.

Hiltner: So that rather than become the bride's wedding it becomes primarily mama's wedding.

Pastor: The minister has a different problem too with frustrated mothers who are displaced in a strange community.

Hiltner: Exactly, and there I leave you on your own! (*laughter*)

Reflection: In an earlier day, when our society was less mobile, a person was born, baptized, confirmed, married, and buried in the same community and the same parish church. There was unity in our liturgical life, an unplanned but nevertheless definite coherence. In an increasingly mobile and transient society, that unity is no more. The church must expend more effort in consciously and intentionally structuring its worship life, partly because we can no longer assume that simply by doing the liturgy as we have always done it people will be able to participate meaningfully.

The above dialogue illustrates some of our problems. In an earlier day, a wedding service performed by a minister away from the couple's home church and hometown would have been unlikely. Of course, during the exigency of World War II or various other unusual situations, couples were often forced to seek out a minister in some faraway place who would quickly marry them before the groom went overseas. But I hear more going on in this conversation than a mere pastoral adaptation to unusual circumstances.

While any pastor can well understand (and even encourage) the reluctance of a young couple to have their wedding turned into "a large social wedding with all the trappings," one suspects that the couples described here may be asking for something else. It is possible, as the pastor seems to intimate, that a couple might desire a small and quiet wedding ceremony somewhere other than in their hometown in order to spare their parents the expense and bother of a large wedding that hometown social pressures might demand. If so, a wedding on so-called neutral ground could indeed be "a very positive kind of thing."

But other issues are raised as the dialogue on this matter continues, particularly in Dr. Hiltner's responses. He assumes that the parents "probably wouldn't permit" a small wedding in the hometown. Such a wedding is described as a "big shindig" where, "rather than becoming the bride's wedding it becomes primarily mama's wedding." The picture one gets here is that of the courageous young couple who, resisting hypocritical social pressures and their parents' wishes, remove themselves from all the superficiality of the "big shindig back home" and marry in the solitude of a church that is on neutral ground in their university town.

Of course, if it is only *their* wedding, then they have a right to be married anywhere they choose. But in our foregoing discussion of the wedding as a liturgical event with communal, pastoral, and educational significance, we argued that if it is only *their* wedding, it is less than a *Christian* wedding. Fortunately, I think the pastor in this dialogue senses this. He expresses a nagging regard for the problems of "frustrated mothers who are displaced in a strange community."

Dr. Hiltner's remarks show a troubling lack of awareness of the needs of parents and, in a roundabout way, a lack of sensitivity to the needs of their children (the bride and groom) in this situation. I question his implicit assumption that the parents, their friends, and their hometown have little to offer the couple except

144

the hassle of a "big shindig." We live in a culture that is strangely infatuated with youth, that questions not only the ability of older generations to transmit values to the youths but also whether any of those values is worth transmitting in the first place. In the interest of pastoral concern for the young couple, it seems that the pastor would at least question the couple's implicit assumption that the "big shindig back home" is of little value in this transition rite. The big shindig and its accompanying rites, rituals, and liturgies (both outside the church and in the church), may be the primary means the parents (and, for that matter, the couple) have of expressing their love and concern, marking off this important plateau in their lives, dealing openly with the positive and negative feelings the marriage evokes, and acknowledging and celebrating the wide range of meanings that surround this life-changing event. The rituals, strange and unimportant though they may appear on the surface, are ways of coping, are carefully prescribed means of helping to confront the difficult and come to terms with the new and the threatening. Pastors, as representatives of the whole church, should remember that they also have a responsibility to care for the needs of the parents. "Frustrated mothers" may not be a laughing matter. The parents, along with the marrying couple, are involved in a rite of passage of their own. In a very profound sense, it is their wedding too.

The pastor might raise the possibility that the couples who meet on neutral ground may be seeking to avoid more than the big shindig. What does the hometown wedding signify to the couple? Simply a superficial social scene or possibly a painful confrontation with their roots, their history, their past relationships, and family? Does the couple adequately appreciate that marriage involves not just the union of a man and woman but also a union with his or her parents? Does the couple sense how deeply significant communal support, intergenerational relationships, and the wider society will be to the success of their marriage? While none of these factors may be involved in a couple's desire to have a small, quiet, wedding on neutral ground, it does seem important for the pastor, as an official of the Christian community and out of genuine pastoral concern and awareness of the historic, pastoral functions of rituals like the liturgy for marriage (and all the extraecclesiastical rituals that surround it), to at least raise some of these issues before the wedding is dismissed as a meaningless big shindig.

The church does not approach events like the union of a man and woman in matrimony, a family's giving of its child to a new life-changing union, the creation of a home, and the possibility of procreation of children, with disinterested neutrality. We have something to say to people in such crises. We have a witness to bear to the faith we hold and that holds us. We have guidance and educative liturgical acts to offer in order that this crisis of transition and change may also be a time of growth and rebirth in union with faith, hope, and love.

VII
Liturgy and Identity: Baptism

As Tertullian said, "Christians are made, not born." Our identity as Christians is not a matter of birthright, natural inclination, or membership in the human race. God has no grandchildren. I may come to the faith "just as I am," but I will not be in and under the faith until I submit to being remade, done over, disciplined, processed, incorporated, initiated, in short, reborn.

So for me to ask the fundamental, Who am I? (an admittedly overworked but apparently unavoidable question for our age) is to raise the question the church should always be impatiently waiting to answer and thereby do its saving work. It is a question that dominates what has become an interminable period of adolescence, a question that invariably lurks behind all other questions people put to a pastor, and a question that has become somewhat of a fixation for modern humanity because we have looked in the wrong places for the answer. It is a question that causes much psychological pain among our people and a question that the church must answer every time we worship—even if the answer is at any point in time unpopular,

147

confusing, too great to comprehend, or shattering to our self-centered pride.

On any Sunday morning the church has many means of speaking to my Who am I? A creed, hymn, sermon, or trip to the Lord's Table may help remind me of what I already know and never cease needing to know. But the principal, primal, initiating, continuing way I experience my identity as a Christian is in baptism—the concern of this chapter.

However, an examination of present baptismal theology and practice indicates that the baptismal font would be the last place in the church for one to expect help on questions of identity. As I noted in a recent article in *The Christian Century:*

> Those who practice infant baptism speak of it euphemistically as "christening," "infant dedication," as a little educative exercise to remind the parents to get the child to Sunday School, or as an insipid, cute, rosebud of an affair all full of kisses and talk that "God loves you and we love you," hoping that the church can get its real business with the child done later in confirmation class or through an adult conversion experience. . . . Advocates of believer's baptism have not done much better. In too many Baptist churches, baptism is an afterthought to the real work of a prior conversion experience, . . . a procedure mainly of value in entitling one to vote in future congregational squabbles. Baptists' claims that they wait to baptize until someone "is old enough to know what it means" demonstrate that human intellectual, rational knowing or human subjective, inner experiencing is primary. . . . Many look upon the confusion in baptismal practice and theology, the relatively low place which baptism now occupies in the life of the church and the lives of individual believers, and come to the conclusion that baptism is about as effective in making Christians as a cincture on an alb is in ensuring celibacy.[1]

In the same article I asked if it were possible that some of our problems with baptism may be not because of its irrelevance and meaninglessness but rather because the word baptism proclaims "is a tough, unpopular word these days." Having observed the studied efforts of my fellow pastors to do everything possible to avoid getting caught in the act of baptizing and knowing from psychology that we usually avoid, deny, rationalize, conceal, mask, and trivialize that which most discomforts and threatens us, I speculated that some of the same psychological dynamics were at work in our rationalization (and therefore trivialization) of baptism. Perhaps we avoid robust baptisms, not because baptism is irrelevant, but because baptism is so painfully, disarmingly relevant.

It also seemed to me that there were pastoral questions involved in our neglect and misuse of baptism. A quote from G. H. W. Lampe stuck in my mind:

Since baptism encompasses the whole Christian life, lack of clarity concerning the meaning of baptism leads to uncertainty all along the line. . . . The more the baptized learn to see their whole life in the light of their baptism, the more does their life take on the pattern of life "in Christ." It is also of decisive importance to pastoral care to say to a troubled human being, "You are baptized," with all the assurance which this implies.[2]

What is that "assurance" the assertion "You are baptized" might bring to our pastoral care of troubled persons?

To answer that question we must inquire into the meaning of baptism, particularly its meaning as the identifying sacrament of the Christian life. But we must start by reflecting upon sacraments. In my opinion, baptism will not again be significant in the life of the church or the lives of individual Christians until we once again affirm what the church has traditionally proclaimed, that (to paraphrase James White) sacraments

149

are *communal events and sign acts through which God gives himself to us.*[3]

For too long we Protestants have been in the grip of what White calls an "Enlightenment" view of the sacraments that regards such events as baptism and the Lord's Supper as human actions we perform in order to help us remember God's actions in the past. Distrusting the ability of the material to be a bearer of the Holy, we have reduced the sacraments to stimulants to sentiment, occasions for self-commitment, memory exercises that aid us in making ethical decisions or theological insights. The Enlightenment view of the sacraments puts primary stress upon the necessity of our worthiness (stated all too often in terms of our *unworthiness*) to participate in the sacraments, of our cerebral understanding of what is going on with the sacraments, and of certain a priori commitments and experiences we should have in order to bring sufficient faith to the sacraments. Primary responsibility in most Protestant sacramental worship is thus placed upon *me*—my worthiness, my understanding, my commitments, my experiences. Little wonder that, when viewed from this perspective, participation in the sacraments elicits guilt, doubt, despair, or avoidance from Christians who see the sacraments as simply one more reminder of their continuing confusion, unworthiness, impotency, and unfaithfulness. Such an experience could hardly be labeled a "means of grace."

In contrast to this human-centered, human-conditioned, Enlightenment view of the sacraments, Christian theology has traditionally asserted that God is the actor, and we are the recipients of what God does through the sacraments. The efficacy of the sacraments does not entirely depend upon us, upon our ability to love God or to lead holy lives. In his infinite love, God has not left us alone. God continually, graciously, gives himself to us and makes himself available to us through touched, tasted, experienced, visible means. This, God does (thank God) in spite of our best intentions. We do not have to (nor, in the final analysis, can we) make it happen. If we be loved and if we be healed and if we be saved, it is first and forever because of God's own active, self-giving, initiating love. As Calvin said: "He condescends to lead us to himself by these earthly elements, and to set before us in the flesh a mirror of spiritual blessings. . . . He imparts spiritual things under visible ones."[4]

Traditionally, both the Roman Church and the churches of the Reformation (at least the heirs of Luther and Calvin—when we have been true to our spiritual forebears) have viewed baptism as God's work. In baptism, God acts in water to enlarge the family of God and to save them through their identification with the crucified and risen Lord. It is our adoption, our assignment of a place and a task in the Kingdom, our ordination as (to quote from what may have been an early baptismal hymn) members of a "chosen race, a royal priesthood, a dedicated nation, and a people claimed by God for his own, to proclaim the triumphs of him who has called you out of darkness into his marvellous light" (I Pet. 2:9 NEB). While baptism undoubtedly calls forth response on the part of the believer, it is always response, *a posteriori*, to the saving activity of God.

This self-giving of God is not only accomplished through symbolic acts and events, but it is also a communal experience. Jesus did not simply bring a message, proclaim a new idea, or urge a new experience. He formed a group. He gathered a community about himself with which he was to have ongoing contact. The current stress upon Jesus as prophet, revolutionary, revealer of the eschatological Kingdom, preacher, or way to self-fulfillment overlooks the fact that he formed a community that saw itself as *his*

151

community, the recipient of his promises, wedded to his death and resurrection, the bearer of his mandate. That mandate, I remind you, was to preach the gospel as a command to repentance and belief. The concrete reality of that command is baptism. There is little distinction in the New Testament between the church's missionary task and its baptizing. Throughout Acts, for instance, to be converted from the past and to be baptized are one and the same (see 8:12, 35; 9:18; 18:8). Faith is a communal experience. Paul assumes that all Christians are baptized (see I Cor. 1:11-17). Matthew's mission command is to make disciples, baptizing, teaching (see Matt. 28:18-20). "Make disciples" refers to the whole mission of the community of which "baptizing" is directed toward initiating the people into the community and "teaching" is directed to those now within the community.[5]

Unlike the Lord's Supper, the New Testament says little about *how* we are to baptize. We have no liturgical rubrics to follow. The New Testament does say a great deal about the rich variety of meanings within baptism: forgiveness of sins, rebirth, cleansing, death, refreshment, resurrection, adoption, light. But there is one New Testament *way* of interpreting baptism to people. The interpretation of the meaning of baptism is always linked to an interpretation of church. Whenever baptism is interpreted to people about to be baptized, it is always spoken of in the future tense, in terms of promises about their "new identity in Christ" they are about to receive. When baptism is interpreted to those who have already been baptized, it is spoken of in the past tense, as a biographical fact of a new identity, a new status as a member of the believing community.[6]

Before the fact of baptism, there is the interpreting of baptism as "promise . . . to you, and to your children" (Acts 3:39a) which calls forth faith and discipleship. After the fact of baptism, baptism is interpreted as a new

152

fact of life, a revolutionary event through which the risen Christ has "qualified us to share in the inheritance of the saints. . . . He has delivered us from the dominion of darkness and transferred us to the kingdom of his beloved Son, in whom we have redemption, the forgiveness of sins" (Col. 1:12-14 RSV).

This accomplished fact of life enables the continuing discourse and lifelong pilgrimage in faith which is sustained by this extrasubjective authenticity. The purpose of both interpretations of baptism is the prevention of the subjectivizing of belief. Here, at this primal, primary point in the faith pilgrimage, there must be no mistaking that there has been an objective alteration of the neophyte's status and that the objective change is effected by the action and presence of the Lord within and through his community. We are dealing here with grace, which is always in danger of being perverted from a gift of God into an individual achievement of the believer. Baptism is an action done to me and for me rather than by me. I can state it no better than did P. T. Forsyth a generation ago:

Baptism is not primarily an act of the parent nor the child, but of the Church, and of Christ in the Church. It is our individualism that has done most to ruin the sacrament of Baptism among us. We get a wrong answer because we do not put the right question. We ask, "What good does Baptism do me or that child?" instead of, "What is the active witness and service the Church renders to the active Word in Christ's Gospel in the Baptism of the young or old?"[7]

The recipient of the sacrament has a relatively simple role in the enactment of this sacrament. The burden is on the baptizers more than on the one who is to be baptized. It makes all the difference in the world whether we see the burden of Jesus' work placed on the recipient of the sacrament rather than upon the doers of the sacrament. It is the church that is commanded to

153

baptize and thereby make disciples. It is the church to which is given both the burden and the resources to make discipleship possible for others. It is the church that must forever take care to believe, proclaim, and interpret the word of grace it bears.

Sometimes I suspect that we in the church trivialize, avoid, and diffuse baptism partly out of our own misgivings and self-doubt about our ability to "make disciples" and partly out of our irresponsibility that is forever attempting to shift the burden of Christian initiation off our shoulders and onto the backs of those whom we are supposed to be initiating into the Kingdom. Witness our arguments over infant baptism. Both the supporters and the opponents of infant baptism have too often focused upon the recipient of the sacrament. Supporters of infant baptism have sometimes argued that "the child must be baptized in order to be saved" so that the rite becomes mechanistic and divorced from the agency of the baptizers. The opponents of infant baptism have complained that the infant's freedom of choice is violated by the rite so that the burden of the sacrament is exclusively upon the person being baptized. In both cases the agency of the baptizing community is ignored.[8]

It is with great difficulty that we set aside our fixation with the recipient of the sacrament. And yet we must if we are to restore a much needed balance to our overly subjectivized and radically individualized theology, liturgy, and pastoral care. Baptism is proclamation and experience of the fact that we are who we are because God has first chosen us and loved us and called us into his Kingdom. To the question, Who am I? baptism responds that I am the one who is called, washed, named, promised, and commissioned.

This is not to deny my free will to act nor to reject the claim that is made upon me. God's action in my behalf through baptism necessitates my response. I have the freedom to reject God's action (though I suppose the church would agree with Augustine that to reject "who I am" and to live under the illusion that I am "on my own" is bondage rather than freedom). Even the act of baptism itself does not ensure my continuance in the baptismal community. My fidelity, my luck, my courage, and my developments in my own understanding will all affect my ability to live a life that is congruent with "who I am." Not everyone who is called puts his hand to the plow, nor does initiation imply (nor need it imply) total personal commitment on the part of the initiate. Once again, the burden of commitment is on the baptizers who are called to show forth God's total commitment to the one who is baptized.

Baptism affirms that if I grow into the likeness of him who created me, if I continue within the fellowship to which I am wedded in baptism, and if I become a functioning member of the Body, it will be in great part due to God's loving actions toward me, for me, in spite of me, through the agency of the believing and baptizing community. I never cease being dependent upon the baptizers.

Thus, to the perplexing question, Who am I? baptism responds: "You are the sum of your relationships. You are not a self-made man as if you existed in isolation from the web of life, the events of the past, and the claims of others. You are not parentless. The discovery of your identity is group product. You have a history that will take you the rest of time to unravel. You are who you are in great part because of the way you were conceived, nurtured, birthed, and loved by the household of faith. This is who you are."

We who have been taught to look for our identity within the dark recesses of our own ego or through our own vaunted and self-serving deeds or by catching glimpses of ourselves while drifting from one transitory emotional experience to the next will find baptism's

155

response to our identity questions somewhat disarming. It is disarming to be told that my identity, my status, my purpose, are given rather than earned. I hate to let go and to be plunged beneath the cleansing waters until I am pulled like a newborn baby from the womb, until I rest only upon the everlasting arms of God's grace. But baptism says I will never be whole until I risk that kind of death (repentance) and birth (conversion).

Practical Considerations

Unlike many of our inherited rituals for baptism, which were often clouded by Reformation polemics and were theologically inadequate, the new rites for Christian initiation (especially those of Lutherans, Episcopalians, Catholics, and United Methodists) make it clear that herein the church is engaged in the formation of new people with lives that are to change in response to God's actions in our behalf. The opening words of the new United Methodist Service of Baptism, Confirmation, and Renewal are illustrative:

Through the Sacrament of Baptism we are initiated into Christ's holy Church. God incorporates us into his mighty acts of salvation, giving us a new birth by water and the Spirit. All of this is God's gift to us, offered without price. Through confirmation and other renewals of the baptismal covenant, we acknowledge what God is doing for us and affirm our commitment to Christ's Church.[9]

The new rites stress congregational sponsors for the candidates as well as more congregational participation in the ritual itself. Their advocacy of more abundant use of water and richer symbolic action give liturgical expression to our earlier definition of *sacrament* as "a communal event and sign act through which God gives himself to us." The inclusion of the Apostles' Creed, a feature of all historic baptismal liturgies but unfortunately omitted from many Reformation liturgies, along with suggestions for pre- and postbaptismal instruction of candidates are attempts to recover baptism as the church's primary rite of identity and to stress the need for true responsiveness on the part of the candidate.

Every celebration of baptism is thus a celebration of each person's identity in Christ. As Aidan Kavanaugh noted in discussing the new Catholic rites of Christian initiation:

The document is concretely specific on who a Christian is. He is not merely a set of abstract yet imponderable good intentions that are essentially incommunicable and subjectively sovereign. Rather, a Christian is a person of faith in Jesus Christ dead and risen among his faithful people. This faith is no mere noetic thing but a way of living together; it is the bond which establishes that reciprocal mutuality of relationships we call communion, and it is this communion which constitutes the ecclesiastical real presence of Jesus Christ in the world of grace, faith, hope, charity, and character.[10]

At the same time, baptism is also a celebration of the identity of the Christian community. It is our charter of existence, a reminder of whose community we are and what we are expected to do.

This is the primary pastoral and theological reason baptism must never be done privately (except in the most extraordinary of circumstances) or without the presence of the worshiping community. Baptism must be a communal event because the identity it confers is socially structured and communally derived. It is an identity that is not only given by the community but that is forever responsible to and dependent upon the community. In baptism the church is saying to the candidate: "You must never again think of yourself as 'on your own.' You are ours, and we are God's. As we claim you and as God claims you through us, so also your new brothers and sisters will make claims upon you. You are now a part of the Body." John Carr of

157

Emory University told me that at his former parish at the end of a service of worship that included the baptism of a baby, a determined seven-year-old came swaggering up to the front and asked: "Where is this baby that belongs to me now? If I'm going to be looking out for him, I've got to know exactly what he looks like." That seven-year-old was starting to understand what it means to be part of church that takes its baptisms seriously.

Likewise, the celebration of baptism must not be abstracted from the worshiping community because that community is always in need of being reminded of its identity as the Body of Christ. That Jesus should make us baptizers is an indication of his confidence in our ability, by his grace, to close the distance between persons; to wash away the artificial distinctions of wealth, sex, race, or class; to form the people of God of those who were "once no people." In baptism the church is saying to itself: "We are brothers and sisters. We are a holy nation; so it is now too late for our petty divisions. We are royalty; so we might as well start getting used to it. We have been remade into a Body."

As pastors, we must exercise more care in our leadership of the baptismal liturgy. Baptism should take place within the context of the congregation's worship, preferably within the context of the Lord's Supper since baptism is the initiating sacrament to the Lord's Table. Membership in the family entitles one to eat at the family's table. Water should be abundantly used so that the full range of rich baptismal symbolism might be made abundantly manifest to all participants. We must overcome our Enlightenment distrust of matter, symbol, sign, and gesture. We know best that which we have actively experienced. Baptism must always be an acted, touched, felt experience. Renewed emphasis upon the active "facts" of baptism like water, oil, candles, special clothing, imposition of hands, and repetition of creeds helps to underscore the objective quality of the rite and thereby provides a much needed corrective to the excessive subjectivism and verbalism of Protestant worship practices. Baptismal sermons, careful prebaptismal instruction, and continuing pastoral reference to the centrality of baptism will also be helpful. Returning to the church's earlier practice of baptismal vigils and Easter baptismal celebrations that restore baptism to the center of the Christian liturgical year, rather than wedge it insignificantly within a Sunday service, will do much to enable the congregation to renew its experience of this "rock from whence you were hewn."[11]

If it is true that the identity question, Who am I? is at the root of many of our people's problems and if baptism is the sacrament of Christian identity, then pastoral care must also include care in our dealings with baptism. Of all the commentators on baptism, I think no one better expressed its pastoral significance than did Pastor Luther. In his *Small Catechism* (IV, 12) Luther stated that baptism

signifies that the old Adam in us, together with all sins and evil lusts, should be drowned by daily sorrow and repentance and be put to death, and that the new man should come forth daily and rise up, cleansed and righteous, to live forever in God's presence.[12]

Luther thus claims that baptism is an objective, life-changing activity that signifies the alteration that has occurred in us by the work of Christ.

But, as Luther is said to have observed elsewhere, "the old Adam is a mighty good swimmer" who doesn't drown easily in the baptismal waters. Our lives are still in tension between the old and the new. Our sin is forgiven, not removed. For this reason, baptism is (to paraphrase Luther again) a "once-in-a-lifetime experience that takes your whole life to complete." Daily we must die to our old selves and rise with Christ. Daily we must learn to rely upon God to do for us that which we cannot do for ourselves. This is why later experiences of evangelical conversions, contrition and forgiveness, and other new beginnings are best described as baptismal experiences.[13] Fortunately, most of the new baptismal rites provide for periodic celebration of baptismal renewal services. We never become too holy or too old to need to die and be reborn, to confess and be forgiven, to be strengthened by the Spirit, and to be reminded of our roots.

But our later, continuing need to reaffirm God's affirmation of us in baptism must never obscure the indelible, once-and-for-all character of the grace we have received in baptism. After we are identified, signed, sealed, and claimed, we can never fully eradicate the mark of God's grace upon us. You can understand why, when old Luther was suffering from self-doubt or despair, wandering through some dark night of the soul and sailing inkwells at the devil, he received great comfort by touching his forehead and saying, *"Baptismatus sum"*—"I am baptized." Remembrance of his baptism brought comfort and assurance because, said Luther, our God is a jealous God who does not willingly share that which he owns, and baptism is a perpetual sign that God owns *me*.

We who have made God's love contingent on human goodness, human response, human feelings, and human understanding need to hear baptism's word of comfort to those in our midst who despair over who they are and to whom they belong. We have clouded our proclamation of the faith with talk about who we *ought* to be when we should have taken our cue from baptism and spoken more of who, by God's grace, we *are*. The faith is always more about what God does for us than what we do for God. We do not always feel like Christians or look like Christians much less act like Christians. The church despairs over the seemingly meager fruit of its labors. It is sometimes enough to make us wonder if we belong to anyone. At such moments in life we, like Luther, would do well to touch our forehead and remember our baptism. Then we might remember that we are God's children not because of what we have felt or done or understood. We are who we are because of what we have heard in God's "word in water." In baptism we have heard God call each of us by our very own name. God has called us. God does not break the promises he has made to us in our baptism. God keeps his word.

Remember Who You Are

A young pastor shared this baptismal experience with me:

Situation: A middle-aged woman came to my study. I knew her to be a member of our church, but only a nominal member. While her name was on our roll she had not attended church for many years nor had she participated in any of the church's activities.

She informed me that she and her husband had divorced. I knew that they had an unfortunate marriage. She also told me that she had decided to make a new beginning of her life, to "start things over again." She blamed her withdrawal from the church on her husband's negative attitude about the church and religion. He had discouraged her earlier efforts to attend on Sunday morning.

"But God has helped me through all of this," she said. "In fact, I feel closer to God now than at any time in my life. I guess you could say that I have had a kind of 'religious experience.' I could not have made it during the past few months without his help." She then expressed how her religious faith had given her the "courage to end the marriage" and had helped her resolve to "begin life all over." Part of that new

161

beginning was her desire to become active in the church again.

"That's why I came to you," she continued, "I want to be rebaptized as soon as possible."

When I explained to her that our church did not rebaptize people, she seemed disappointed. All of my efforts to convince her that "you do not need to be rebaptized" were to no avail. She was determined to be rebaptized. It seemed very important to her.

Then I suggested that what she might want was a renewal of her baptism. I showed her our denomination's new *Service of Baptism, Confirmation, and Renewal.* I explained that this was designed to enable people to rededicate themselves, to recall their baptism in a public way without getting into rebaptism and the questions that it raised. She was pleased. "The service is just what I had in mind." We decided to do the service the next Sunday since I would also be baptizing a baby then.

I must say that none of us will soon forget that service. When the time came in the service for the baptism of the child, our youth choir sang "I've Passed Through the Water." Then, with the parents and grandparents of the child gathered around the font, I baptized the baby. After baptizing the baby, I announced that we had someone in the congregation who wished to renew her baptism. She came forth, stood in front of the congregation and beside the font. Repeating the words of the service, I said, "Remember your baptism and be thankful," sprinkling some of the water from the font upon her. I then asked if there were others who wished to renew their baptismal vows. The entire congregation stood. Walking down the aisle, I sprinkled, or "aspurged," the whole congregation saying, "Remember your baptism and be thankful." I then said: "Members of God's family, I commend to you this new Christian

whom we have this day baptized and also our sister
————, who has been away from us for a time but
never lost from us. She returns home and has today
affirmed her baptism. Let us welcome them."
We then prayed the concluding prayer:

> We give thanks to God
> for the faith he has worked within you.
> We pledge to you
> our Christian love and hospitality
> as fellow stewards of God's grace.
> Together with you and all Christians
> we seek the unity of the Spirit
> in the bond of peace,
> that in everything God may be glorified
> through Jesus Christ.

There was a moment of silence, then the congregation spontaneously surged forth and embraced the baby and its parents and the woman. It was quite an experience.

Reflection: I see this as an excellent example of a skillful attempt to merge liturgical and pastoral concerns, letting the two perspectives inform each other within the worship life of the community. The Christian faith has much to do with new beginnings. It is important that we be able to recognize and affirm the new beginnings people experience in their lives, helping them to interpret these experiences within the context of the community of faith and its tradition.

This woman had participated in the ending of a marriage. The pastor may have wished to probe a bit deeper into whatever feelings, memories, regrets, relief, or resignation she may have had after ending this unsuccessful union. This is a new beginning for her, but she is not completely new, for she is the sum of past relationships and deeds. Her ability to make significant changes may be partly dependent on her ability to deal honestly with that past. The minister might have suggested that she explore some of that past, not with the intent of arguing her back into the marriage nor with the desire to question her claim to a genuinely fresh start, but rather from a pastoral concern to enhance her "conversion" (if we may be so bold as to use so theological a word) by helping her lay hold of her past.

But in one very real sense, the pastor did challenge her desire and her claim for a completely "fresh start." He resisted her request for rebaptism. While he may have done so out of purely legalistic, denominational considerations, he does have the weight of the church's theological tradition behind him. *Rebaptism* is a liturgical non sequitur because baptism is a once-and-for-all event that, like physical birth or death, cannot be repeated. If baptism is a purely human sign for something we do—our decision, our promise, our commitment—then I suppose baptism can be repeated since we are forever falling away from our decisions, promises, and commitments. If, as classical Christian theology has maintained, baptism is an act of God through the church and if God never falls away, then God's action in baptism need never be repeated. Baptism is a sign of the promise of God, and God does not break his promises. To repeat one's baptism would be to say, in effect, "God lied, I was not adopted, I was not upheld by his grace, I did not enter the family." This, we do not wish to say.

For if baptism is to bring comfort to us, if it is to stand as a lifelong, never-ending, firm assurance of God's claim upon us, then it must be seen as unrepeatable, indelible, objective evidence of that

164

claim. Baptism must stand as a mark of identification that endures upon us, sometimes in spite of us. Therein is a person's true freedom and assurance. And the church seems pitifully short on assurances of any kind these days.

What I hear the minister in this case saying is: "You do not need rebaptism because, even if you have drifted from God, God has always been there for you. You were away from God's family, but that family always considered you as its member. You are not so much making a completely fresh start as you are returning to where you began. A child may wander from the parent, but that child never stops being the parent's child. You may have forgotten your baptism, but you never lost it. You are who you are by virtue of your baptism, and now you are simply returning to claim who you have always been. Remember your baptism, and be thankful."

The service itself showed keen pastoral sensitivity to the woman's need to publicly, ritually acknowledge her "homecoming" as well as the congregation's need to publicly, ritually reclaim its own responsibility for her. By placing her baptismal renewal in the context of another baptism, the pastor beautifully illustrated the lifelong nature of baptism and its relevance for the vicissitudes of the faith pilgrimage. The use of the ancient practice of asperging helped to make this event an experiential, tangible occasion, rich in symbolic content and emotion.

I like the bold liturgical claim of God's claim upon us that I see in this pastor's dealings with this woman, and I hope it suggests ways of caring for persons by opening up the heritage that is ours in baptism. May the church search for new ways to help all of us remember who we are by helping us all to remember the effusive, graceful waters of our baptism.

VIII
Liturgy and Community: The Lord's Supper

You have heard it said that the family that prays together stays together. I say to you that the family that *eats together* stays together. There is much biblical evidence to support my claim that the simple act of eating together is a primary means of familial unity.

Could the contemporary breakdown of many of our families be attributed to our families' so rarely eating together? Frozen dinners eaten while staring at the six-thirty news, fast-food rush orders gulped down on the way to somewhere else, junk food and snacks that enable us to avoid confronting one another at table—little wonder that love and unity are difficult for us. We cannot share something even so basic as bread.

And if mealtimes are basic for the unity and maintenance of human families, how much more basic is this table fellowship for the family of God. Something sacred happens to people who have shared food and drink. Across all cultures and faiths, the act of eating together is a universal sign of unity and love. Jesus knew this. One need only recall the progression of meals in the Gospels in which he ate with saints and sinners to be reminded of the centrality of table fellowship and the symbolic power of sharing food and drink. It is no accident that Jesus' disciples knew him best and saw his truth revealed most dramatically "when he was at table with them . . . in the breaking of the bread" (see Luke 24:28-35 RSV). Nor is it surprising to find the early church, when it gathered for Sunday worship, gathered not in the temple but at the table.

Recently I led a worship workshop at a large, decaying, downtown church. When asked to list the problems within their congregational life, the lay persons in the workshop listed "coldness, unfriendliness, anonymity, lack of feeling." After I talked about the Lord's Supper, its centrality in Christian worship, its biblical significance, and its role in worship renewal, a number of the lay persons said that they would like to see Communion celebrated more frequently in their church. The group was on the verge of recommending monthly celebrations of the Lord's Supper to the church's administrative board when the pastor entered the discussion. "Now, wait a minute," he said. "I'm afraid you don't understand this church. We are a big, impersonal, downtown church. Our members don't know one another personally, and, frankly, I doubt if many of them really want to know one another. They come from all over the city to be here. I think what most of them want is to come in here, sit down, hear some good music and a good sermon, and then go home. All this fellowship stuff just isn't appropriate for us."

I noted that while the pastor spoke, the lay persons were all gazing at the floor, seemingly hoping to avoid my asking their reaction to their pastor's assertion that all the congregation wanted was "some good music and a good sermon."

"Well, I'll take your word for it," I responded. "But what if this church wanted to get the congregation together for some big project? What if, for instance, you wanted to raise a large amount of money for a new educational building? How would you go about it?"

"We did that a few months ago," responded the man who was chairman of the finance committee. "After making plans for the building and determining how much we would need, we had a big congregational dinner one Sunday after church. We all gathered in the fellowship hall, had dinner, saw a slide presentation on our church—"

"Wait a minute," I interrupted. "What does eating together have to do with raising money?"

"Well, you know how people are," answered the layman. "There's something about having the whole congregation sit down for dinner. They get a good feeling about the church. They get to know one another. It breaks the ice."

"Yes," I said. "You know how people are. So perhaps Jesus knew what he was talking about when he told us that we ought to 'do this,' this eating and drinking, when we get together in order that we can really get together."

The Lord's Supper, Communion, has much to do with the expression and the formation of community. In our present hunger for community, we should never forget that the central, historic, constitutive, communal act of the church has been its celebrations of the Lord's Supper. As indicated in the last chapter, while sacraments like Baptism and the Eucharist are primarily communal events and sign acts through which God gives himself to us, sacraments can also be adjuvants to pastoral care. As Paul Pruyser says, "Sacramental occasions . . . lend themselves to personal contact at some level of depth, to preparatory counseling, to special personal scrutiny of motives, emotions and states of belief or doubt."[1]

In this chapter we will focus upon the Lord's Supper

as a means through which the risen Christ forms the Christian community and as an occasion whereby the pastor can not only minister to people's search for community but also better understand why community often eludes us.

A Biblical Example

Lack of community was at the heart of the problem in Corinth. First Church Corinth was a fragmented church (see I Cor. 1:1-12). Even the gifts of the Spirit had become a source of division rather than unity (see I Cor. 12). It was in this context that Paul wisely turned to teaching about the Lord's Supper as a means of healing Corinthian brokenness, giving us our earliest exposition of the Eucharist in the early Christian community (see I Cor. 11:17-34).

Paul begins with an appeal to memories of the patriarchs (see 10:2-4). The Eucharist is a work of deliverance and of community formation similar to the work of God in the Exodus. The dangers of the wilderness (idolatry, dissention, magic) are even now with God's people. Even though the Fathers were "baptized" in the sea and ate the "spiritual food" and drank the "spiritual drink," they were "overthrown in the wilderness." Their behavior after eating the "sacramental" manna was a sin against the graciousness of God. Remembrance of their punishment should be a warning to us (see 10:6-13).

Then the table of the Lord is contrasted with its opposite: the "table of demons" (see 10:14-15). Satan attacks most viciously where Christ is most present; so there is much at stake in the matter of our eating. The problem of "food offered to idols" (see vv. 19-30) is not the food itself, for all food is a creation of God (see v. 26). The problem is "not partaking with thankfulness"

(v. 30), letting scruples about eating divide the community, allowing the Body to be torn by arrogant, self-seeking individualism.

Starting at chapter 11, verse 17, Paul specifically discusses Corinthian abuses of the Lord's Supper. The divisions Paul notes elsewhere have even corrupted the Eucharist (see v. 18). Some eat and drink to drunkenness while others are shamed because they have nothing to eat. "When you meet together, it is not the Lord's Supper that you eat" (v. 20), Paul tells them. They have invalidated their Eucharist by factions, selfishness, and humiliation of others. They have despised the common life and, in so doing, they have failed to "discern the body" (v. 29). The "body," of course, does not refer to the elements of Communion here but rather to Paul's favorite analogy of the church as the "Body of Christ" (Rom. 12). The Corinthians' problem is not, as Leitzmann once suggested, that they do not take the Eucharist with enough seriousness. Their problem, as Conzelmann contends, is that they misunderstand that the focus of Communion is not upon some magical, heavenly food but rather upon Christ and their brothers and sisters around the table who have been saved, called, and gifted by Christ and formed into his "body." They fail to "discern the body," thinking that this meal is similar to the sacred meals they may have eaten in their former pagan rites where one achieved personal immortality by gulping down as much "heavenly food" as possible.

The abuses arose

because the Corinthians were crude sacramentalists (along the lines of the mystery religions). They thought the sacramental food was a substance. Each ate for himself. This pneumatic individualism destroyed fellowship. Paul does not appeal to the Corinthians to recognize the sacramental significance of the saving food—they do that already. They should rather understand that the sacrament takes place in the context of the church and is thus to be actualized by the realization of their community.[2]

Paul tells them that the Lord's meal is a different kind of religious meal, even as Christianity is a different kind of religion. The sacramental reality is the act of table fellowship. *Koinonia* is the test and the result of true *eucharistia*. The "real presence" of Christ is in this assembled worshiping community, formed by virtue of Christ's death and resurrection.[3]

In their misunderstanding and lack of vision and compassion, the Corinthians eat a selfish *idion diepnon* ("your own meal") and not the communal *kurakon diepnon* ("Lord's Supper") and thereby eat and drink the judgment of God upon themselves (see v. 29). And this judgment is not some future reckoning, it is present judgment, present in their weakness, sickness, and death (see v. 30). Every time they eat in the Lord's name, their so-called Lord's Supper becomes a blasphemous act, a symbol of their brokenness, and a judgment upon their failure to be unified members of "the body." In the next chapter Paul goes on to speak about "spiritual gifts" and their place in "the body," climaxing his thoughts, in chapter 13, with his immortal "Hymn to Love."

Comparing Paul's eucharistic theology with some of the historic arguments over the liturgy yields interesting insights. He never mentions the qualifications of the celebrant, correct formulas, or rubrics. Nor does he posit the saving power of the Eucharist in the mere repetition of a command of the Lord. Its power is in the quality of the Christian life lived through the community with Christ as its head and we as its members. This communal, ethical, political understanding of the Lord's Supper not only contradicts the medieval concern over the confection of a sacred object through the formulas and procedures of the Mass but also the subjectivism and self-centered "me and Jesus" individualism that fragmented later Protestant worship. For Paul, the Eucharist is not some little private pact between Christ and the individual believer—the social behavior before, during, and after the meal is decisive.

We are forever tempted to try to turn this nonobjectifiable act of formation into a pagan, magical, objectified, institutionalized substitute for our own "transubstantiation" into the Body of Christ. We are forever forgetting the ethical dimension of the Christian sacraments as well as the sacramental basis for our Christian ethics. But every time we approach the Lord's Table, the health of our community judges our Communion, and our Communion helps to form our community, even as it was so for the Corinthians. We are called forth from our rugged individualism and self-centered concern and into the Body. In this sense the Eucharist is the norm and the pattern for all Christian worship, a sign-act through which Christ gives himself to us and thereby forms community of most unlikely individuals.

Communion as Constitutive of Community

While the Christian liturgy has an undeniable appeal to Kierkegaard's "solitary individual" and our corporate worship is always in danger of demanding that the individual unwillingly submerge him or herself into a totalitarian corporation ("You do it *our* way or get out"), the history of the liturgy shows that fragmentation has been a greater problem for us than excessive corporation. In the Middle Ages, the separation of clergy from laity, the dissolution of the Mass into a priestly performance while the congregation engaged themselves in private devotions, votive Masses, extraliturgical devotions, individual confession, and a host of other developments fragmented "corporate worship" into individual devotions. In spite of the efforts of the major

172

Protestant Reformers, this tendency toward individualism was continued, even accentuated, in Protestant
worship. Cranmer's *Book of Common Prayer* was designed
to promote truly *common* worship with the people as
active participants. But often the result of prayerbook
worship was liturgy that reinforced individualism with
each worshiper's staring at the printed page, sitting,
reading, listening rather than actively participating.

Protestant churches within the Puritan or Revivalist
tradition tended to focus upon the individual, seeking
to elicit individual commitment, enthusiasm, conversion, or understanding. Public worship was conceived of
as the activity of a conglomeration of individuals rather
than a corporate experience. Rationalism, subjectivism,
and individualism characterized every facet of Protestant worship. There is no more vivid symbol of this
fragmentation than the widespread custom of using
individual wafers (or cubes or pellets) for the eucharistic
bread and individual glasses for the chalice. Concern
over hygiene seems to have overcome celebration of
community. Each one (as Paul would say) "goes ahead
and does his own eating." Or is this excessive concern
over hygiene simply a means of transferring our
misgivings about community and succumbing to our
fears that we will be unable to form community? We will
have more to say about this later.

Faced with the historic tendency of the community's
worship to fragment and centrifuge, Paul's assertion
that the Eucharist is not only an expression of the
quality of Christian community but also a vehicle in
forming that community may strike us as a rather naïve
theological affirmation.[4] Paul is making a theological
affirmation (through the Eucharist, the risen Christ
forms community), whether it is a naïve or unrealistic
affirmation remains to be tested within the community's
actual experience of the Eucharist. But Paul is also
making, at least from the point of view of this study, a

functional observation about the Lord's Supper. A significant amount of psychological and anthropological data indicate that liturgical events like the Eucharist can indeed be a means of community formation.

Psychological study indicates that personalities change and mature most easily in a supportive environment that encourages them to experiment with new patterns of behavior.[5] While the relatively safe, structured, patterned environment of corporate worship will undoubtedly attract some dependent persons who use the supportiveness of group worship for regression rather than growth, liturgy can provide a setting for risk and innovation within the personality—group and individual personalities. Public worship is always an invitation to the individual to risk communion, to move out from oneself into the larger body; but it should be an invitation given within an environment where refusal to accept the invitation is always permissible and forced togetherness is avoided.

Ritual gives us safe boundaries and a supportive setting from which to venture forth into new modes of behavior. The daily ritual of shaking hands when we meet a stranger helps us through the crisis of meeting and makes introductions more comfortable. One of the major tasks of parents is to teach their children the myriad of rituals through which we order our lives and relate to other people. Erik Erikson, in a fascinating essay on the adaptive functions of rituals during infancy (i.e., the ritual of a human mother greeting her baby in the morning), speaks of ritual as a means of fostering a sense of "separateness transcended."[6] A child who is deprived of these all-important rituals of relationships in infancy, according to Erikson, may have difficulty in forming and sustaining relationships in later life. Without learned, experienced rituals for meeting and relating to others, a person may suffer from impulsive excess and promiscuous relationships on the one hand or overly compulsive self-restriction on the other, social anomie or moralistic repression. Thus, rituals for meeting and affirming one another are indispensible. Erikson says that such early rituals provide the psychosocial foundation for an inner equilibrium that psychoanalysis calls the "strong ego," able to make deep relationships with others without annihilating the individual self. Rituals for meeting provide the invitation, the means, and the boundaries for our community.

The Lord's Supper is a ritual for meeting. It gives us a form, a ritual for acting our way into patterns of behavior, behavior that may elude us when we "act naturally." As Howard Clinebell has noted, "It is easier to act your way into a new way of feeling than to feel your way into a new way of acting." In the actions of the Meal, an individual who feels isolated and unaccepted may discover the possibility for community and incorporation. Ritual, purposive, patterned behavior is the universal means of providing group cohesion and continuity. Anthropologists speak of "rites of intensification," periodic ceremonials relating to the life of the group and its shared beliefs and symbols. Through these celebrations a group intensifies commitment to its particular set of meanings and values, and individuals become rehabituated to patterned behavior. A network of relationships is forged among participants, and common loyalties are reinforced.[7] In its common rites such as the Eucharist, the Christian community not only speaks about its values in abstract ideas and concepts, it attempts to embody these meanings in the mind, heart, and behavior of its people. Meanings become concrete, alive, intense, and compelling through the drama of ritual, and they are given a sense of permanence through repetition.

Every time the congregation gathers, it acts out the essential features of how the world is supposed to be. For example, in the Byzantine, mosaic-encrusted churches of Ravenna, interior art and sacred liturgy unite to form "a new heaven and a new earth," a reconstructed cosmos where our eyes are opened and the lordship of Christ is made manifest. I am thinking here of the church of San Appollinare in Classe or the Orthodox Baptistry in Ravenna where one withdraws from the essentially unreal world outside the church where sin, death, and chaos reign and enters the "real" world where God is "making all things new"—even us. In this way, the church's art and liturgy functioned to convince worshipers of the validity of the church's vision and to deepen their faith that the vision could become a reality. Withdrawing to worship was not seen (as some contemporary "secular" theologians have tried to depict it) as a withdrawal from the "real" world into some fantasy world of faith. Worship invited us to enter a sacred space to do sacred things so that we might better see what is most real. As Leo said of the Lord's Supper, it "makes conspicuous" who we really are and are meant to be.

In creating an environment in which common values are intensified and realized and structured patterns of behavior are repeated, ritualized events like the Lord's Supper become an invitation to community. Psychotherapist Margaretta Bowers notes:

The anxiety of the separateness, of the aloneness of the individual is lessened as he enters into the ritual—dancing, singing, moving together, sharing food and drink. He loses his sense of differentness and becomes one with the common identity of the group. He emerges from the ritual more comfortable in his security as a member of his group, sharing common symbols, common customs, a common god; and he rebounds from the regressive experience with greater maturity, with that courage called faith.[8]

William Hulme reminds his fellow practitioners of pastoral care that the reconciliation people so desperately seek is communicated through phenomenological involvement. The Lord's Supper is a sacrament of reconciliation. As such it is a healing antidote for guilt and estrangement; however, the Sacrament has suffered from the distortions of an individualistic piety. . . . The trend was either toward the assurance of personal forgiveness and intimacy with God or toward the individual reception of sanctifying grace. These are no longer predominant emphases. In their stead is the corporate significance. . . . It is not the individual believer who receives from the Lord but the fellowship of believers, who receive also from each other.[9]

Another way ritual becomes an invitation for growth and change is by providing an occasion for "ecstasy." *Ecstasy,* which literally means in the Greek to "stand outside of oneself," occurs within any religious ritual that is worthy of the name. Part of the power of ritual is its sameness, its patterned predictability. This sameness is helpful in that, by rhythmically engaging ourselves in familiar ritual, we are freed for moments of true spontaneity and ecstasy. Part of the value of well-defined and familiar ritual is that we do not have to think about it. We loose ourselves within the familiar words and gestures so that our minds are free to roam and play in unknown territory of the psyche. Our mind wanders to the important things we usually do not have time or courage to think about. In these ecstatic moments, the tight grip of the status quo is relaxed, our cynicism is playfully challenged, and we are free to move and breathe and envision alternatives.[10] We stand outside ourselves in order to better see ourselves. We become detached from the rigid confines of everyday life in order to catch a glimpse of life as it might be lived. We put on costumes, act out different roles, and try out new patterns of behavior. We "make believe," for instance, when we come to the Lord's Table, that we are not really strangers but brothers and sisters. We see a vision of life beyond the imprisonment of today's facts. The breathing space that is provided in ritual is essential for the growth and change that are prerequisites for community.

In *Toys and Reasons,* Erik Erikson notes the common adaptive significance of children's play and adults' rituals. Both childhood play and adult ritual provide us with a place apart from daily social progression and the daily, predictable assigned meanings that surround us. The adult's rituals and the child's playpen give us a circumscribed world of make believe for children or the ideal, or what-could-be world, for adults. In both situations it is a world of illusion, of something that is and is not real at the same time. In calling the ritual world one of illusion we are not drawing a line between truth and falsity. Illusion, from this perspective, is a necessary psychosocial structure through which we are given a space to sort out the divergent stimuli that press upon us and the divergent handed-down meanings that have been given to us. There is no time, no space, no room to make sense of our world without play and ritual.[11] An illusion is that on which we project ourselves and our hopes so that we might better see ourselves in order to grow. Many of our religious rituals are cast between the tension of a world in process and the fixed, certain world that is. A ritual can only be helpful to us as it maintains a healthy balance between these two poles. It is thus a servant of human adaptability to an often threateningly ambiguous world. It helps us encounter a new world without fully owning that world, a new selfhood without fully relinquishing our old self. Out of such experimental, playful, ritualized encounters comes the opportunity for creative adaptation and growth.

An example of how the ritualized, active, participatory, invitational aspects of the Eucharist can aid in the formation of community is the use of the ancient "kiss of peace." This ancient gesture, reintroduced into the liturgy after centuries of neglect, has troubled some modern worshipers who see it as the introduction of a frothy togetherness into what was formerly a solemn and transcendent service of worship. In fact, the Peace greeting is not an occasion for touchy-feely conviviality; it is an act of faith. In the earliest eucharistic liturgies, the Peace appeared at the end of the opening Service of the Word as a seal of what had taken place. The Word had reminded the assembly of who they were. Now they gave their active assent to the Word, confirming Goethe's dictum that "the highest cannot be spoken; it can only be acted." The mutual embrace was a gesture that confirmed the mystery of Christ's presence and the people's unity with the risen Lord and with one another. Implicit in this exchange was the intent to reconcile any differences among the members of the Body, before you "come . . . and offer your gift" (Matt. 5:23 NEB). Gradually, the Western church came to explain the Peace primarily as a gesture of mutual forgiveness, reconciliation, and communion rather than as a seal or bodily acted "amen."

In the Middle Ages, as eucharistic theology limited the presence of Christ only in the consecrated elements and in the ordained clergy, the laity were omitted from the gesture. When the Peace became a stylized act reserved for the clergy, it was accompanied by a further lack of appreciation for the mystery of the Lord's presence among his assembled people. In a short while, the Eucharist was "performed" without even the necessity of a gathered congregation, and the Peace became a meaningless anachronism.

Can the primitive awareness of Christ's presence in the community be recovered? In the new eucharistic liturgies, every time the Peace is shared, it represents an act of faith that we can overcome our differences, that the hearing of the Word and celebration of the sacrament will bring faith that enables us to leap over our self-imposed boundaries. People are invited to risk and reach out and touch.[12] A congregation's ability to participate in this gesture of peace may be an indication of the quality of its life together and its ability to risk itself in worship. This may not come naturally, nor need it. It comes as a gift, as grace from the One who gathers us. A pastor reported to me that his congregation perfunctorily passed the Peace every time they celebrated Holy Communion for over a year, each person dutifully turning to his or her neighbor, forcing a weak handshake, perhaps an amiable word, but that was all. Then, at the Christmas Eve Eucharist, after reading the Christmas lessons and preaching on them, as the offering was received, the pastor said something like, "Tonight the Prince of Peace is being born among us, light is coming into our darkness; let us therefore rise and exchange signs of love and peace." The congregation exploded; people moved about embracing one another, embracing the minister, and sharing a special kind of fellowship. From that night on, the pastor reported, every time the Peace was passed, that same kind of unity, spontaneity, and warmth permeated the act. "I think it took them a year or so to figure out what was going on, to give it a try. I think they were surprised that they liked it. I'm glad we stuck with it until the time was right," he said. I am also pleased that this pastor "stuck with it," continuing to offer this resource to his people until they were able to accept it. They kept going through the motions until they got it right. The Peace helped them to do what they wanted to do but would not have been able to do without this ritual invitation for meeting. It was also a concrete reminder of the limitations and shortcomings of their community until it could be made whole. "How much easier it is to limit belief in the Lord's presence to bread and wine or to the priest who handles them" rather than to risk ourselves at the mercy of His incorporating love.[13]

It is the very essence of a sacrament that it is not only a

series of ritual acts and gestures but that it is also a bundle of symbols. We Protestants have historically been distrustful of the nonverbal and the symbolic. Our liturgical iconoclasm resulted in worship that is verbal, rational, and symbolically inadequate. Fortunately, recent developments in Protestant worship have sought to restore some of the ancient symbols. The early church understood the evocative, expressive, formative power of the symbolic. Christian rites were full of talk about light and darkness, body and blood, death and life. The Romans accused them of being "cannibals," thinking that their rites bordered on the vulgar. Bread, wine, and water, the stuff of everyday life put in an ultimate context, became the symbols around which Christians gathered themselves.

In *Totem and Taboo*, Freud noted how the Christian Eucharist resembles the totemistic feasts of many other religions that speak of eating the God and incorporating the deity into the worshiper's body. Generations before, the early church Fathers, in referring to the Eucharist, had told their congregations that "you are what you eat." Freud, who had a rich appreciation for the psychosocial implications of our eating habits, would have agreed with the Fathers. Freud speculated on the possibly destructive and often adaptive function of these primal symbolic acts of eating and drinking in a religious context. As we argued in our earlier reference to Freud, it is unwise to view these primal symbolic actions as only the result of neurotic patterns of behavior. While worship symbols may function in the exercise of obsessive-compulsive behavior in some individuals, these symbols also have a creative and adaptive significance for the great majority of people who come in contact with them. Through our symbols, we visually express the verbally inexpressible; we plumb the very depths of the human psyche and enter into that dim, normally inaccessible region where dreams, myths, and visions are formed. Sacramental worship engages our most primitive instincts. The central symbols of the Eucharist—bread, wine, cup, cross, body, blood—hold archetypal power. Its themes speak to the deepest substrata of our being. It involves all of our nature: the subconscious, the sense, feelings, memory, mind, and will. In this encounter with the symbolic, fractions within the self may be expressed and then healed. We may find our views of reality broken down and then reconstructed. Symbols are thus not intended by the religious community to simply soothe the anxious person but to intensify and expand the awareness of God within people. This may well heighten our anxiety as the archetypal symbols beckon us to handle the untouchable and to enter the holy of holies where both demons and gods reside and deep calls unto deep.

Symbols, like the bread and wine of the Eucharist, not only evoke, invite and express, they also form. We build our universe around certain shared symbols. The one who wields symbols, who works in the symbolic, exercises power. No one who witnessed Hitler's mass rallies in Nuremburg stadium with thousands of chanting, saluting Nazis rotating around the twisted cross can easily dismiss the formative (and, in this case, often demonic) power of the symbolic. This is why those who are charged by the Christian community in the explication, preservation, and utilization of its fund of symbols must take great care in how they administer those symbols.

Sometimes, as I have observed the almost studied efforts of my fellow pastors to ignore, defuse, or botch the central symbols of the Eucharist, I have suspected that many of us may subconsciously feel that if we trivialize these symbols, they will go away. How many of us have tried to convince ourselves and our congregations: "It's *just* bread." "It really doesn't matter how we do the ritual since it is *just* a symbol." "This is *merely* a symbolic way of acting out what we believe in our hearts." Sometimes this appears to be a kind of whistling in the dark before the threat of the numinous. Our glib casualness bespeaks our inability to lay hold of this elemental power that has called us forth—an inability perhaps arising out of our fear of being engulfed by that power. Lacking the ability to use the symbols of our faith, we lack the ability to approach the numinous without fear of being destroyed by it. Since we have no boundaries for our dealings with the Divine, no focus or place, we avoid the Divine lest in meeting it we should be devastated by it. We tell ourselves, "This is *merely* a symbol," and go on about our superficial busyness.

As Tillich once said, a symbol is not *merely* a symbol. Something may be *merely* a word, or contain *merely* literal truth, but nothing is *merely* symbolic.[14] Every time the pastor leads the congregation in the Eucharist, we affirm the efficacy of grace that comes through ordinary, everyday objects like bread and wine, eating and drinking, and people. The congregation itself, if Paul is correct, becomes a symbol of the "real presence" of Christ. As we celebrate the incarnation of God in our midst, these symbolic actions evoke a power among us, putting our human assembly in the context of the sacred, calling forth a depth of reality that would otherwise be unavailable to us without the presence of the symbols and their attendant symbolic actions.

I think the church recognized the formative power of our worship rituals and symbols when it claimed, *"Lex Orandi, Lex Credendi"* ("the rule of prayer preceeds the rule of belief"). Historically, liturgy preceeds and forms our theological affirmations. Practice preceeds doctrine. We pray first; we speak about the meaning of our prayer afterward. The pastor must therefore exercise astute care in "reading" the symbols of our faith, in opening up the evocative power of our liturgical symbols to the faithful, and in guarding our essential symbols lest they be crowded out or diffused by alien symbols. Today's liturgical symbols will not only form tomorrow's theology but will also help shape tomorrow's community. When individual, minute, "fish food" wafers are used in place of a hearty loaf of bread and when (as in my own Methodist tradition—since the 1920s) watery grape juice replaces blood-red wine, one need not wonder why our popular eucharistic theology is weak and meaningless and Communion within our community is a dry, lifeless nonevent. How could it be otherwise?

It was not always so for the church. Consider the not-so-minor matter of the eucharistic bread. The offering of the bread was originally an important action, symbolizing the people's offering of the stuff of everyday life. "It is your own mystery which is placed upon the Lord's table; it is your own mystery which you receive," Augustine told his flock as the bread was laid upon the Table. "Because there is one bread, we who are many are one body, for we all partake of the one bread," said Paul (I Cor. 10:17 RSV), seeing the bread as a symbol of Christian unity. John Calvin continues the bread-unity symbolism, paraphrasing an ancient prayer from the *Didache* (9:4):

As the bread which is hallowed for the common use of us all is made from many grains so intermingled that it is impossible to distinguish them from one another, so ought we to be so united among ourselves in an indissoluble friendship, and what is more, we receive there one and the same Body of Christ so as to be made members of it.[15]

The fraction of the bread, the placing of the bread in the people's hands, the very acts of baking, breaking, tasting, smelling, and eating the bread have all been focused upon at various times as symbols of deep mysteries of our faith, mysteries and experiences that remain ethereal and unaccessible without the sacrament.

In the Middle Ages, as the eucharistic elements were gradually taken away from the people, the church seemed to sense that its bread symbolism would need changing too. In stressing the transcendence and remoteness of God, the church began to adopt unleavened bread as a sign of purity and incorruptibility. A suitable, pure, unspotted offering was demanded. A levitical understanding crept into the Christian Eucharist. The bread became holy, special food to be handled only by the priest. Ordinary, everyday table bread, the bread of joy and fellowship, bread that bore the unmistakable stamp of the human hand, was rejected. In so doing, the church removed itself and its Eucharist from the powerful symbol of God in the presence of the ordinary and the everyday, of the acceptability of our fallible human offering, and of the sign of the unity of God's people. The very bread upon the table became a statement about the fractured, inadequate ecclesial consciousness of the congregation.[16] Or did the practice of using special, unleavened bread precede the church's modified definitions of eucharistic presence? At any rate, the use of priestly bread went hand in hand with the view of the Eucharist as a priestly rite. The symbols and the theology were mutually dependent on one another. Therefore, the nature of the very bread upon the Table is of no small consequence to the community's celebrations. In concerning themselves with the rituals and symbols of the liturgy, pastors are being true to what we know about human nature and humanity's need for ritual and symbol as well as the incarnational nature of the revelation of God in Jesus the Christ.

In our quest for communion and community, let us gather at the Table in the hope that we will be gathered by the One whose presence makes the feast, in the hope that our eyes will be opened and that we will see him standing among us, that our *eucharistia* will foster *koinonia*. Hear Augustine as he invites us to the Table *and* to the Body:

> The faithful acknowledge the body of Christ when they are not ashamed to be the body themselves. . . . That is why the apostles explain the meaning of this bread to us with the words: "We who are many are *one* bread, *one* body." (I Cor. 10:17) O sacrament of love! O sign of unity! . . . Whoever seeks life can find a source of life here. Let him come forward and let himself be incorporated, and he will be given life. Let him not shrink back from the binding of the members to one another. . . . Let him hold on firmly to the body.[17]

A Case

"Let This Cup Pass from Me"

Situation: I had been asked by the pastor of a small, inner-city church (composed mostly of older people) to lead a workshop on Holy Communion. The pastor had been attempting to improve the congregation's Communion services during the past few months. He had introduced a number of innovations in the order and mechanics of the service that had been well received. However, he had experienced frustration in his attempts to get the congregation to use a common cup for Communion (they had been using individual Communion glasses). Even when he compromised on his original intentions and suggested that they at least use the "intinction method" with the common cup (dipping the bread into the cup rather than drinking from the cup), he was dismayed to find continued resistance to the idea. I followed his suggestion that, during the workshop, I discuss the biblical, historical, and symbolical value of using the common cup and loaf in Communion in hopes that they would consent to the idea. At the end of the workshop, we sat in the

186

church fellowship hall discussing what further changes they would like to see in their church's celebration of the Lord's Supper.

Me: Can you think of anything else you could do to make Communion a more meaningful experience for people here?

Member 1: Well, I heard somebody say that he thought it was beautiful when we used the one cup and the one loaf rather than the little glasses and wafers.

Member 2: No, I can't go with that! I heard just the opposite of what you seem to have heard.

Pastor: *(Speaking to Member 2)* What do you mean?

Member 2: I mean that lots of people just don't care for that business of everybody drinking out of the same cup.

Pastor: Well, that wasn't even what we did. Nobody drank from the cup. We just dipped our bread into it— *(Looking at me)* What do you call it?

Me: Intinction?

Pastor: Yes. Intinction. I can't figure out what got people upset over that.

Member 1: I guess they were afraid of catching a cold or something. Some people are funny about that kind of thing.

Member 3: Yes. I do remember somebody saying that they didn't like all that touching and dipping. The woman who mentioned it to me said that she wasn't coming again when we have Communion if we're going to do that. She said she thought it was repulsive.

Pastor: *(To Member 3)* Is that how you feel?

Member 3: I didn't mean that I cared one way or the other. As far as I'm concerned, it doesn't make any difference whether we do it one way or the other. It's just a matter of mechanics.

Pastor: But I thought somebody said he liked the cup.

Member 1: Well, I did. But it's not a big deal for me. I don't want to make anybody uncomfortable. It's just a nice symbol. The important thing is not how you do it but what you feel inside.

Member 3: Well, Lord knows we've had the sickness here this winter. I can't really blame people for not wanting to risk catching something. The people I talked to really didn't like it. One told me to be sure to say something about it.

Me: Did anyone find the use of the common cup and loaf to be a meaningful experience? something worth keeping?

(Awkward silence)

Pastor: Well, you all know how I feel. I like it. I like it for some of the same reasons Dr. Willimon has given. I think we need more unity in our church, more fellowship, and I see this as a symbol of that. I think people get something out of it.

Member 1: Well, I just hate to upset people. Some people are set in their ways.

Member 3: The thought of everybody handling the bread and all does sort of get to me. I'll admit it.

Pastor: I just hate to see us get so hung up on germs and forget the real meaning of Communion. But if this is how you feel, I think we at least ought to have a common cup and loaf on the table. As a kind of symbol. We can use the glasses and wafers but keep the symbol of the cup and loaf. How's that?

Member 3: Well, that's O K. I think that would be nice. The real point is to focus on Jesus rather than on the mechanics anyway.

Member 1: Maybe folk will gradually change, and we can do the common cup thing sometime. But I suppose it's not all that important anyway.

Reflection: The Lord's Supper is not only an invitation and a means of body-building and community formation. It is also a judgment upon the limitations of our Communion.

In this case study we have a pastor who longed for a

unified, visibly joined, worshiping community. Undoubtedly, his own pastoral ego was involved in his desire to, in effect, "make" Communion for his people. (No less than the ego of the visiting "worship expert" who sought to sell the congregation on proper liturgical form!) One can feel his pastoral exasperation ("That wasn't even what we did") and his attempt to use the outside "expert" ("What do you call it?") to push his people into the new worship form and into a new sense of community. The common cup and loaf became symbolic of the pastor's own eagerness to achieve "more unity in our church, more fellowship." While his desire to foster deeper Communion was admirable, it has a curious resemblance to some of the popular medieval attempts to "make" Eucharist and "confect" the Mass through miraculous priestly initiative. While it is obvious that I would heartily agree that better attention to the symbols of the Eucharist would enhance its community-forming power, community ultimately comes as a gift of God and as the result of the freedom and the risk of individuals who venture forth into Communion rather than as the achievement of pastoral coercion or manipulation. The pastor is ultimately frustrated in his desire for unity through common cup and loaf—the "real meaning of Communion" as he sees it. He is at least able to assert his wishes through the placing of the cup and the loaf on the table "as a kind of symbol," even though they will play no integral part in the actual Communion and will stand there as stark reminders of Communion that was not to be.

But the lay persons' discussion shows that the pastor is not alone in his yearning for communion and community. Member 1 initiates the talk about community, albeit in an oblique way, but remains concerned throughout the discussion that the group not "make anybody uncomfortable" or "upset people." Member 1's comments show the tragic dilemma in which we in the church are often trapped; we want Communion but not if the path to Communion necessitates conflict. We long for the invitation to touch, to be made whole, to be healed but not if, in that process, our limitations and inadequacies are exposed. In the end, Member 1 retreats, assuring himself and the group that "it's not all that important anyway."

Members 2 and 3 represent their remarks as only their faithful relaying of other people's opposition to the worship innovation. At various points the pastor confronts Members 2 and 3 ("Is that how *you* feel?"), pushing them to claim and to be honest about their own feelings in the matter. They generally evade him ("I didn't mean that I cared one way or the other") or else continue to present themselves as simply attempting to represent and care for the feelings of others ("I can't really blame people for not wanting to risk catching something"). Finally, Member 3 admits that "the thought of everybody handling the bread and all does sort of get to me." In a congregation of older people, health and hygiene are understandably central concerns. But excessive self-concern, whether over questions of health or anything else, becomes a hindrance to the more abundant life, an alibi for all shortcomings. It is interesting that we often present our anticommunity feelings in the guise of deep concern for the trampled feelings of individuals within the community. In so doing, those who attempt to encourage and prod us into community are often made to look as if they are insensitive to the rights and feelings of other people. If communion is to happen, confrontation cannot be avoided since our exclusiveness, our self-concern, our self-centeredness, must be confronted if we are to die to our selfishness and rise to community.

That confrontation, in spite of the pastor's attempts

to encourage it through his participation in the conversation and through his focus upon the symbols of Communion, is avoided (1) by transferring the conflict to questions of hygiene while at the same time dismissing the hygiene issue as a meaningless eccentricity of some people (Member 1), (2) by attempting to minimize the symbols question as "just a matter of mechanics" (Member 3) or as "not all that important anyway" (Member 1), (3) by deflecting the focus of the symbol from the congregation and its limitations "to focus upon Jesus" (Member 3) as if focusing upon Jesus would relieve the congregation of its uncomfortableness at not being able to form community. The discussion ends with conflict between the pastor's hopes and the people's limitations unencountered and unresolved, with Member 1 (who initiated the discussion in the first place) plaintively hoping that "maybe folk will gradually change, and we can do the common cup thing sometime." Then, as if to give a final, ambivalent, but unconvincing blessing upon their conversation, he assures himself and his fellow Christians, "But I suppose it's not all that important anyway."

This group is left with many unresolved barriers, problems, yearnings, and conflicts, and yet (like the first disciples before them), even in the midst of those unresolved problems at the Eucharist, Jesus both invites and enables them to gather. We do not have to "get it all together" first. He is forever inviting us to be at Table with those whom we are not yet ready to be with. Our hesitance and ambivalence to enter this table fellowship are similar to our predispositions before any meal to which we are invited.[18] People have expectations, hesitations, and frustrations about meals that are not unrelated to our reactions to the Eucharist. Will I be a good host? Will I enable people to have a good time? Will I have a good time? Will the other people who are invited like me? Will I drink or eat too much and make

191

a fool of myself? Should I bring the children? Will I be forced to sit next to so-and-so? Can I act naturally? Will I be served something I don't want to eat? Will the food make me sick? Will I be bound afterward to any commitments? These are also the fears, ambivalences, and conflicts we feel when we gather for the Lord's Supper.

In fact, the dynamics of the group's conversation are strikingly similar to those of the table talk at the Last Supper with Jesus and his first disciples in the upper room. There, at table, at the only meal in Luke in which Jesus is the host, the dispute over greatness (see Luke 22:24-27), the accusation and betrayal (see Luke 22:31-34), the denials, doubts, and conflict, show that the disciples neither understand Jesus nor are they ready for the community he has promised. Like the Corinthians after them, they betray the Lord by the very brokenness of their life together.

And yet, the point of the story is that it is *these* disciples; in all their fear, self-doubts, ambivalence, and conflict; whom Jesus invites to dinner and promises a place in his Kingdom. Throughout the Gospels Jesus only eats with hungry, needy, bickering, knowing, and unknowing sinners. We are more like those first disciples at the Table than we know or are willing to admit. In the Lord's Supper, he takes the most common and matter-of-fact elements of any community and breaks them and blesses them so that they might be used for the edification of the Body. We may not be the best material for community, but it is *his* community, and he chooses the elements. It is *his* body, and he calls forth the members.

Sometimes I wonder if we make this the Lord's Supper because it is too threatening to make it ours. We focus on Christ as if he were some sort of external phenomenon, far removed from the ambiguities of our fleshly existence. We will not have him "where two or three are gathered together." It is too close for comfort. We turn it all back to dead history, making the meal a "memorial" so we can stand back and look back and watch him go through the risk of union and communion so we will not have to risk it ourselves. We objectify and sanctify it so we will not have to make the "passover" into his Body. One suspects that devotion to Jesus is thus used as an escape from the complexities of becoming community. We either focus upon the elements of bread and wine and transform them into sacred food or we dismiss the elements as "just symbols" and focus upon germs or our own feelings or our doubts rather than stretch out our hungry hands and receive.

In so doing, our so-called Lord's Supper is experienced by many people as only a painful reminder of all that we are not. Our talk about love, unity, communion, sounds like blasphemy. Like that unused, untouched, unfilled chalice and that uneaten loaf of bread the pastor left upon the church's Table, the Eucharist becomes a symbol of our inability to come and be filled, our utter unworthiness to "discern the body." The meal becomes a way of avoiding communion rather than receiving Communion. The meal becomes hollow and uneventful because there is no "real presence" of the gathered community. People sense that people are gathered, but few are really present.

Or perhaps the Eucharist is more than simply a painful testimony to our failures at communion. The bread is not only broken, it is also blessed, offered, and given to those who are hungry enough to eat. The Lord's Supper stands not only as a reminder of what we are but also as an invitation to what we can be, by his grace. Perhaps our fears over the cup, over the loaf, over the table fellowship, are our way of expressing our more basic fear that we will be unable to form community on our own. But we are not "on our own." The Eucharist reminds us, shows us, that if we be fed and if we be joined and if we be nourished and thus mysteriously grow into his likeness, it is only through his grace. It is he who is the host, who calls us and feeds us and ecstatically takes us outside ourselves in order to do for us what we cannot do for ourselves. In saying yes to him and his invitation, we say yes to our true selves. Hear Augustine again in his familiar Communion sermon, giving an invitation we can never recall too often as we come to the Table:

"You are the body and the members of Christ." If, then, you are Christ's body and his members, it is your own mystery which is placed on the Lord's table; it is your own mystery which you receive. It is what you are that you reply Amen, and by replying subscribe. For you are told: "The body of Christ," and you reply, "Amen." Be a member of the body of Christ, and let your "Amen" be true.[19]

IX
Liturgy and Leadership: Priest and Pastor

In its perennial attempt to find an easy cure for what ails it, the church frequently decides that its seminaries are the root of its problems. While it does my own professorial ego good to think that we in the seminaries are exceedingly influential over the life of the church, I doubt that we can be given too much credit for either the church's triumphs or its failures. But on one occasion when one of my clerical brothers was haranguing seminaries for allegedly ruining the church, he made the mistake of suggesting that "some of these seminary professors need to get out of the classroom and back into the pulpit a while to see what things are really like." A colleague of mine at the seminary who could take no more of these attacks rose to his feet. "Brother, let me assure you that we know all too well what things are 'really like' in our churches. For we are at a better vantage point than even the pulpit. We sit Sunday after Sunday in the pew."

I suppose that I wrote this book as a result of having to

195

spend more time in the pew than in the pulpit for a while. From this vantage point I was able to see not only the level of liturgical leadership of my fellow pastors but also my own leadership problems reflected in them. What I saw was not very pleasant. "Why," I had to ask myself, "do we pastors continually inflict our congregations with poorly prepared, poorly delivered sermons when any lay person will tell you that (at least in Protestant churches) preaching is primary? Why, when a pastor is before more people in Sunday morning worship than at any other time in the week, do we mumble through vague, poorly constructed, almost inaudible prayers; slouch around the altar as if we were fixing a washing machine rather than making Eucharist; chatter incessantly about nothing throughout the entire service, and, in general, appear to go to great lengths to give people the impression that we are doing nothing of any consequence, leading them nowhere of any great importance, and dealing with material of no particular significance?"

Our casualness with the Holy, our sloppiness with the liturgy, are not missed by lay persons. When I talk with laity about worship, they continually express bafflement at why their pastors seem to invest themselves within every other pastoral activity besides the leadership of public worship—the one pastoral activity every pastor is expected to be able to do and the activity the lay persons themselves continue, in every study I have seen, to rank at the top, or at least near the top, of all pastoral activities. I have also found that many ministers, no less than their parishioners, are baffled by their own devaluing of and lack of investment within worship. What is the source of our timidity, hesitance, avoidance, sloppiness, and general lack of attention to the Sunday morning gatherings of our people?

Undoubtedly, the sources of this problem are

complex and multifaceted, related to our perception of ourselves as individual pastors, our understanding of the church and its ministry, our evaluation of our individual strengths and weaknesses, our assessment of our people's expectations, and a host of other psycho-social-theological factors. In earlier chapters of this book I mentioned the failure of Protestant seminaries to adequately equip pastors for their role as worship leaders and the traditional lack of interest on the part of Protestant pastoral theologians and church leaders in the area of worship. I also noted the lack of appreciation for the power of the liturgy in forming and transforming the people who worship, a lack of confidence in the efficacy of the liturgy in guiding, educating, sustaining, reconciling, and healing people, and a lack of sensitivity to the centrality of the liturgy within the life and witness of the church. This book has attempted to speak to those concerns, attempting to sensitize pastors to the power and the promise of the church's worship.

But I suspect that problems with the pastoral leadership of the liturgy may have deeper roots. While it is important, very important, for each pastor to adequately articulate a sound liturgical theology, to know something of the history of the liturgy, and to have some practical skills in how to lead worship; even knowledge and skills do not appear to be enough. Why is it, I have had to ask myself of late, too many of my fellow pastors know all the "facts" of worship, show personal gifts and abilities in their activities outside of worship that should make them excellent worship leaders and yet still seem unable to lead worship? One suspects questions of ministerial identity, role confusion, and authority may be at the root of the problem.[1] In other words, a major source of the problem for many pastors is inadequate understanding and experience of ordination—the concern of this final chapter.

197

Ministry as a Function of Community

In recent discussion of the ordained ministry, I sense confusion stemming from fuzzy definitions of the "priesthood of believers" principle, based upon the "royal priesthood" image that is applied to God's people in I Peter 2:9. In chapter 1 we noted that, while all Christians share Christ's high priestly ministry to the world by virtue of their "ordination" at baptism (see chapter 7), this does not mean that there is no need or any basis for the development of the role of the ordained priesthood. While we Protestants affirm the "priesthood of all believers" in the sense that I Peter speaks of it, we do not thereby claim that this eliminates the need for an ordained ministerial office. I am unimpressed with much recent thought on ministry which wrongly attempts to support the ministry of the laity ("the priesthood of all believers") by detracting from the need for an ordained ministry. In fact, one reason few lay persons feel like "priests" to one another and to the world is that they so rarely see or receive "priesting" from their pastor. I have yet to see a dynamic, committed church with a vibrant lay ministry that is not led and challenged by the dynamic, committed, vibrant ministry of some pastor who knows that his or her ordained ministry is the essential sign and focus for the shared ministry of all Christians within that congregation. And it makes no difference whether that ordained person is called priest, pastor, or preacher.

The theology of ordination has at its heart "the simple fact that priests (pope, bishops) are and function as officials of the Christian community."[2] All our pious accretions, talk about a special aura of holiness, shamanism, alleged virtues and skills, and undue reverence for the community's ordained representatives are only distractions from the simple fact that the

198

ordained ministry is a function of the Christian community. An ordained minister is an official of the community, a representative, a designated leader. With my Protestant heritage, I recognize that an ordained minister should be, must be, called by God. That call from God should be personal, experiential, and received and responded to with some degree of specificity. I know of no good pastor who cannot point to some time in life in which he or she was led to say yes. But with Calvin, I recognize a "twofold call" to the presbyterate. God calls us, and the church calls us. While the explication of and reflection upon God's call to the priesthood is a worthy subject for study, here I wish to emphasize the call of the community, because I sense that it is the currently neglected aspect of our ministerial identity. An ordained minister is an official of the community. It does not advance our understanding of the ordained minister's role to say that it is God's action in and through the minister that is the central factor in his or her functioning. God is involved in the ministry of all Christians. It does not help to claim that the minister's training and expertise are the central factors in his or her functioning. It can be readily demonstrated that the clergy's current attempt to claim "professional" status and expertise are not particularly relevant to either the historical claims for ministry or to the community's current perceptions of what it needs from its ministers.

No, the central matter is in the office, in the officialness of the ordained minister's activities. To put it bluntly, there is no difference when a priest baptizes, preaches, forgives, blesses, prays, counsels, or supports compared to when any other Christian does these things—save in the officialness of the action. The difference is only in the official character of the ordained minister. The Service of Ordination, in whatever tradition it occurs and whatever form it takes,

199

is simply, but also most significantly, the conferring by the community of that official character upon certain designated individuals. God may have designated the persons *a priori* to the community's recognition. But without that community authorization, all individual claims for officialness are unrecognized and therefore invalidated.

I choose to speak of the ordained minister by the rather mundane term *official* in order to lay out, in as stark a manner as possible, the Christian community as the source of our authorization as priests. To speak of the priesthood in an "official," functional way runs counter to the humanly unrealistic and theologically unfounded expectations some of us have of our priests. Some of us have claimed that priests are different from the run of "average" Christians in a spiritual sense. This alleged "specialness" has taken many forms of late. Henri Nouwen speaks romantically of "the Wounded Healer" as if suffering and empathetic sensitivity were somehow the peculiar domain of the priest. Urban Holmes speaks mysteriously of "sacramental persons" who, "not only in word but in their very person, embody the Christ" thereby incarnating "the expectancy of the transcendent with the immanence of the personal."[3] Talk of this kind betrays a kind of insecurity on the part of the clergy and their self-appointed defenders, a fear that if we speak of the clergy as "officials" of the Christian community, we will do away with some "essential" quality that somehow makes them "special." We act as if officialness alone were not enough, not exciting enough for leadership, not dramatic enough to deserve the lifetime call of God.

Other writers on the ministry have used other images in hopes of retaining that priestly "specialness" even if they are unwilling to speak in our present age of some special "spiritual sense." Writers within the area of pastoral psychology, when they have turned their thoughts toward a consideration of the basis for the ordained ministry, have tended to speak of ministry in terms of the possession of certain skills, information, and professional functions. In his *Ferment in Ministry,* Seward Hiltner declared that the main cause of the current "crisis in ministry" was pastors' need for more skill in doing what they do, "functional responsibility" as he called it. Hiltner defined that function mainly in terms of pastoral care and counseling skills. A host of books by Lyle Schaller urged ministers to accrue skills in organizational analysis, administration, planning, and goal setting.[4]

The logical culmination of all this was a popular book by James D. Glasse, *Profession: Minister.*[5] If a "professional" is defined as a person who possesses certain knowledge and skill, who has certain institutional commitments and standards, then, Glasse contends, a minister deserves to rank alongside other professionals.

While the call to skilled competence and mastery of certain exclusive disciplines of the clerical "profession" has an appeal, particularly as a way of legitimizing Christian ministry before the goals and standards of the secular world, one strongly suspects that the call to professionalism represents a rather questionable attempt on the part of the clergy at self-legitimization and self-justification by using currently popular secular standards of efficiency and competence. This is troubling, not only because it tends to be at odds with historic, theological bases for the ordained ministry in its new claim for "specialness" by virtue of certain skills and abilities *apart from* the community's bidding and authorization, but also because it succumbs to a pragmatic, utilitarian, self-serving position that is today the greatest tragedy of two of our major "professions"—medicine and law. The very "professionalism" doctors and lawyers so jealously guard has removed both of these professions from the community and the people who need their services the most and has contributed to a producer-consumer mentality the clergy would do well to avoid. Richard Neuhaus makes a helpful distinction in his criticism of the professional model for ministry: Anthropologists, in their study of so-called primitive societies, sometimes distinguish between the role of the magician and the role of the priest. Magicians offer certain expertise to a clientele. Priests participate in a community. You go *to* a magician—in our society he may be called doctor or lawyer—with a particular problem to be fixed. You *belong* to a community of which the priest is an agent of the community's identity and ministry.[6] The call to the Christian ordained ministry is a call to the priesthood of the community, not to the performance of magic. The priest lives to serve, not to be served.

While the emphasis on officialness can be caricatured to raise the specter of petty bureaucrats, functionaries, organization men, and dull little people who are sanctioned by a mediocre institution, the stress upon office does have the advantage of removing us from old and new debates over some *character indelebilis,* sacred or professional "specialness," or other individualistic claims for ministry, to a fresh consideration of the most basic source and purpose of the priesthood. I note that the New Testament shows no interest in our debate over the "validity" of our orders. The New Testament does seem to raise the issue of what orders are for. What divine purpose is being worked out through the officialness of the pastor? To what good end is this office directed?

Officials are neither desirable nor necessary for any community except for the realization of the community's purposes, the pursuit of communal goals. All groups designate leaders, in all manner of formal and informal ways, not to make leaders but to make a group. Leadership is not an optional matter for a group,

202

particularly a group that wishes to perform any significant task. Jesus knew this. Jesus not only preached, healed, judged, and released; he formed community. He empowered a group to turn the world upside down. He commissioned and sent forth in order to enlarge that new community. He was, George McCauley reminds us, not so naïve as to think that a vision so bold as his could be sustained without an organized community. He therefore organized, brought together, joined, and outfitted a community. Individual personalities emerge in the Gospels only as reflective of the community that is being formed.[7] Priests are not to be so much "in orders" as "under orders." The vision of Christ is a political, social, worldwide vision of body formation, "that they all may be one." Georges Bernanos' country priest caught a glimpse of that community-wide vision the ordained minister is under orders to nurture:

My parish! The words can't even be spoken without a kind of soaring love. . . . I know that my parish is a reality, that we belong to each other for all eternity: it is not a mere administrative fiction, but a living cell in the everlasting Church. But if only the good God would open my eyes and unseal my ears, so that I might behold the face of my parish! The look in the eyes . . . these would be the eyes of all Christianity, of all parishes—perhaps of the poor human race itself. Our Lord saw them from the Cross.[8]

The priest, from the earliest times of the church, was the one who was designated by the community to share and represent Christ's community-wide vision. The concentration of the priest is upon the community forming as well as community criticizing dimensions of the faith. As stated in chapter 1, edification is the burden of his or her particular vocation to the ministry. The pastor is the one who is charged with seeing—in all aspects of pastoral care—individual lives within the context of the whole; to bear the sometimes heavy burden of the community's tradition; to note the presence of inequality, division, and diversity; to create the conditions necessary for consensus; to foster a climate where reconciliation can occur; to judge the potentially demonic aspects of our "togetherness"; to ask whether the community we seek and attain is a specifically *Christian* community; to distinguish between his or her personal preferences and what community cohesion, maintenance, and critique require.[9]

Admittedly, others in the community may do all these things and may even do them better. But it is particularly significant when an ordained minister does these things because that is the priest's job. Yes, his job. Charism, skill, good looks, sensitivity, intelligence, may make the priest better at the job, but none of these characteristics is the origin, source, or rationale for the job. Members of the community recognize the community dimension, the concern for the Body in its past, present, and future state as the job of the priest. Their recognition gives significance to what the priest does. They also recognize that the community dimension is placed upon the shoulders of the official on a standing basis, as the priest's specific concentration and burden. Whatever community-building skills or perceptivity others in the community may have is not acknowledged by the community in the same way as those of the pastor. This is the pastor's job. He is expected to care for the community by virtue of the office. The pastor is authorized, however inarticulately or haphazardly, by the community in this job—with no disrespect for the competence of others.

Without that authorization, the job of priest or pastor is impossible. If the pastor neglects his community-forming role, assumes that someone else can do it, and gets sidetracked into being a counselor of individuals, a changer of society in general, an independent biblical scholar, or some other similarly individualized task, sooner or later the pastor will be driven back to the communal dimension. If not, the pastor will never discover his or her uniqueness and identity as priest.[10]

Because of its officialness, one cannot become priest by private fiat. People who are confused into thinking that the call to the priesthood is simply a call by God addressed to an individual conscience are invariably disappointed when the community fails to recognize their officialness. Failing to receive the official authorization of the community, they may seek official standing in some subgroup of the community where they can lead those of similar ideological persuasion. But this ends in cliques, sects, or faddish partisan movements that are invariably less than the fullness of Christian community.[11]

Admittedly, the presence of the priest or pastor does not guarantee community. But his or her presence does guarantee a visible, personal reminder that community is desirable and that common concerns are paramount to individual ones. The very presence of the priest is a testimony, an invitation to community. Other fellow Christians may chiefly concern themselves with their own struggle as individual Christians. The priest cannot indulge in such individualized concern. He is a community person by virtue of his ordination. Through the priest, people come to see their individual religious striving as membership in a community, as common enterprise, interrelationship, mutuality, as continuous with the struggle of saints in the past, and linked with other Christians who "at all times and places" have called upon the name of the Lord. "It is the *community perspective* that the priest announces by his presence in sacramental situations. And it is that perspective that the community supports when, through ordination, the community receives a new official into its midst."[12]

Show me a church where there are fundamental questions over ordination, and I will show you a church in the throes of fundamental conflicts over community. In its conflicts over ordination, a church must be given credit for realizing that its response to ordination questions will be determinative of its community.

The burden of the ordained ministry (and it is always more burden than privilege) is that priests and pastors have the vantage point from whence to get a firsthand, official view of the lack of community, the difficulties of community, and the separateness within the community they serve. Most pastors have nagging doubts about what they are doing in the midst of an apparent noncommunity so full of division. Those doubts may be a sign that the pastor is about his or her business, standing in the middle of the tension between our rugged individualism and Christ's call to community.

But if a priest or pastor doubts the *desirability* of community or the *possibility* of community, then that is another matter. In the face of that kind of doubt, the priest will attempt to obtain self-fulfillment through control of others or through false prestige or worldly power, falling into paternalism and authoritarianism and thereby assisting the laity in avoiding their responsibility for community. Or the preacher will abandon the community's book (Bible) and take his text from some other source that is more vague and less prone to judge the limits of our self-conceived "gospel." Or the pastor will attempt self-justification by putting impossible leadership demands upon himself, thinking that he must be a super-Christian, a superempathizer, a superdoer of good works, a paragon of faith and virtue, a better practitioner of the priestly arts than the laity ("super apostles," Paul called them in II Cor. 11:5 NEB, RSV). In so doing, the pastor not only diverts people's vision from the Body but also sets himself up for becoming the scapegoat for the people's failures at community. After all, since their pastor has helped them to dispose of both God and the community, who else do they have to blame?

The Service of Ordination is that rite of the church that sets apart some people for the crucial yet modest function of helping the community to gather and then to be edified. All Services of Ordination are clear in their statement and demonstration that they are creating an official of the community. They will invariably claim the presence and work of God in the ordination. But that presence and work is not for the creation of some larger-than-life Christian or some mysterious guru. It is for the purpose of community formation. As the bishop addresses the ordinand in the new *Book of Common Prayer:*

the Church is the family of God, the body of Christ, and the temple of the Holy Spirit. All baptized people are called to make Christ known as Savior and Lord, and to share in the renewing of his world. Now you are called to work as a pastor, priest, and teacher. . . . As a priest, it will be your task to proclaim by word and deed the Gospel of Jesus Christ, and to fashion your life in accordance with its precepts. You are to love and serve the people among whom you work, caring alike for young and old, strong and weak, rich and poor. You are to preach, to declare God's forgiveness to penitent sinners, to pronounce God's blessing, to share in the administration of Holy Baptism and in the celebration of the mysteries of Christ's Body and Blood, and to perform the other ministrations entrusted to you.

In all that you do, you are to nourish Christ's people from the riches of his grace, and to strengthen them to glorify God in this life and in the life to come.

My brother, do you believe that you are truly called by God and his Church to this priesthood?

Ordination rites are also clear in the source of this community builder's officialness. The laying on of hands, a historic gesture symbolizing the transference of power, the gift of the Holy Spirit, and the commissioning of someone by the community, are part of every ordination rite. The candidate for ordination may be asked some questions about the facts of the faith and his or her own personal predisposition toward those facts. The candidate may have gone through some process of education and skill acquisition. But the sacramental, symbolic focus of the Service of Ordination is always upon the laying on of hands as a sign of the bestowal of officialness by the community of faith.

In most rites of ordination, the symbols of that officialness will be presented to the ordinand. A stole, an ancient Roman symbol of rank which came to symbolize the yoking of the priest to Christ and his church will be placed around the person's shoulders. A Bible, the church's book, the repository of the church's tradition, will be presented. A eucharistic chalice and paten will then be given to the new priest. These will be the priest's tools of the trade in the work of community formation and edification. The new pastor is now equipped, by virtue of the community's designation, to identify the Lord's people by baptism, to be host at the Lord's Table, to wait upon the Lord's people, and thereby to help form them into the Lord's Body. Through the rite, the church proclaims the source and the purpose of its ordained ministry.

"Take thou authority to preach the Word and administer the sacraments," the bishop says to the ordinand as he or she is presented with the Bible. These words are both command and promise. The new priest may boldly take authority because authority has been so boldly given. The command is to "take." While the community's gift of officialness is prior to the candidate's reception of the gift, unless the ordinand assumes the new role that is being given, then the community's offer of officialness is void of meaning. The promise is this: When one dares to take the community's offer of authority, one will be confirmed by God in the fruits one's ministry yields.

Within the seminary, in working with future candidates for ordination, I have often noted reluctance to "take thou authority." Students will sometimes speak of their humble desire for the church to "treat me like anybody else," to "respect me as an individual person." These wishes, they will come to see, are not possible to grant. "Anybody else" and "individual persons" will be of little help to the community in its task of becoming the Body. In some of our current fuzzy thinking about the "ministry of the laity" and the need for pastors to "just be themselves," I suspect that a subtle evasion of the command and the promise of ordination may be at work. We ministers sometimes wish to God that we could be "just one of the boys—or girls" so we should not have to bear the burden of being a community person. Our desire to be like anybody else may stem, not from our egalitarian humility but rather from our stubborn, self-centered pride that recognizes the threat of linking our personhood to the community's will. Some of our agonized doubts about our own lack of ability and our unsuitability for the demands of ministry may be rooted in our inability to accept the gift of officialness when it is offered to us. Our doubts about ourselves as ministers may stem, not so much from our doubts about our own personal attributes (for, as we have said, personal attributes are secondary considerations in ordination; the community's attributes are primary) but rather from our doubts about the ability of the community to bestow authority and the ability of God to empower and form community through us.

These doubts and misgivings about the validity and efficacy of our officialness will invariably be expressed in our leadership of the community's worship. For in the leadership of worship, the community function of the priest is revealed most clearly, the source of the priest's officialness is affirmed most strongly, and a pastor's self-understanding will be laid bare for all to

209

see. Lay persons are correct in assuming that their pastor's leadership of worship is the primary and revelatory pastoral activity. They know enough to sense that if the pastor cannot be helpful to them in the leadership of the community's worship, the pastor will not be of much help to them elsewhere. If the pastor cannot be of service as the presence of Christ's community-wide vision, then the pastor will be unhelpful in their fulfillment of their individual vocations to become members of that community-wide vision.

Some Practical Observations
on Pastoral Leadership of the Liturgy

Some time ago I was seated next to a woman at a dinner party who, in the course of the evening's conversation, told me that her congregation had just been sent a new pastor. "How do you like him?" I asked.

"Oh, he is wonderful," she replied enthusiastically. "He gives the best benedictions."

I confessed that I had heard many compliments of ministers' abilities, but that was a compliment I had never heard. I asked her to explain.

"Well, we had never thought much about benedictions. Perhaps we had never really had one. But the first Sunday he was with us, at the conclusion of the worship service, rather than rush back to the door to greet everyone, he stayed at the front and said something like: 'Now I am going to bless you. I want you all to look at me and receive my blessing because you may really need it next week.' We all watched as he raised both hands high above his head, stretching out as if to embrace us, looking at each one of us, and almost like a father, blessing us in the name of the Father, and of the Son, and of the Holy Spirit. His benedictions have become the highlight of each Sunday as far as I am concerned."

In a way, I think that woman's testimony says all that I

wanted to say here. Her testimony on the helpfulness of her pastor's blessing reminded me of a fine essay Paul Pruyser wrote a few years ago on "The Master Hand: Psychological Notes on Pastoral Blessing."[13] Pruyser noted the potential usefulness of this ancient gesture as a means through which to "dedicate the individual to the divine providence." Pruyser was disturbed at the halfhearted way in which many pastors pronounce benedictions within the worship service and speculated on the possible reasons pastors avoid this powerful symbol of providence. First he noted that the decay in the performance of pastoral benedictions coincided with the erosion of the classical theological doctrine of providence. Was this erosion due to poor theological instruction on providence, or due to poor demonstration of divine providence through the pastoral blessing? Perhaps people found it difficult to conceive of divine providence because they had never experienced that providence through another human being—their pastor.

Another possible reason was given for the poor performance of benedictions by pastors. It is very close to the major concern of this chapter. The second possible reason lay in the pastors' own conflicts concerning their professional identity:

When worship leaders perform sloppily in their liturgical work, they are obviously not attributing a high professional value to this part of their activities. And when they perform badly in benedictions, the unspoken messages to the congregation are that: (1) benedictions are rather meaningless, (2) the pastor does not deem the people worthy of receiving them, (3) the pastor himself has long given up thought of providence, or (4) the pastor refuses to shoulder the shepherd's role.[14]

The poor performance of significant liturgical gestures like the benediction, indicates that the pastor may have let his own misgivings about his ability to bless overcome the community's authorization of the pastor as the one to whom is given the power to bless. By refusing to bless, the pastor shows insensitivity to or lack of knowledge about the needs of people. The pastor also shows that he or she may be so consumed by his or her own conflict about authorization and competence, or need for self-fulfillment and self-understanding that the pastor cannot respond to the needs of others. Ordination reminds us that the pastor blesses not because he or she has answered all inner questions about divine providence, not because the pastor does it better than anyone else in the community might do it, and not because the pastor may feel the personal need at that moment to do it but because the community has bestowed upon the pastor the job of doing it.

In fact, as Pruyser goes on to suggest, by merely attempting to do the job of blessing right, the pastor may find that his or her own doubts and misgivings are assuaged by the very action of the performance itself. Liturgical gestures are psycho-dynamically so important and are so closely tied to the inner emotions, that performing the proper motion may very likely stimulate the corresponding emotion. In blessing, the pastor may be blessed. But whether or not the pastor is blessed (an entirely secondary matter to the pastor's job), it is important for the pastor to get out of the way, so to speak, and be willing to function for the community that is always in need of such blessing. I suppose this is what C. S. Lewis was thinking about when he complained somewhere, "The modern habit of doing ceremonial things unceremoniously is no proof of humility; rather it proves the offender's inability to forget himself in the rite, and his readiness to spoil for everyone else the proper pleasure of ritual."

I am reminded of an actor friend of mine who

surprised me by going on stage even though she was sick with a high fever and felt terrible. "They paid their money," was her reply when asked why she did it. "They didn't come to the theater tonight to see me or hear about my aches and pains. They came to be in the presence of the genius of Ibsen, to be entertained and renewed. My job is to act. My bad feelings have nothing to do with it." Of course, the acting analogy can be taken too far when applied to the leadership of the liturgy, but I think it does help remind us of the source of our officialness and of the purpose of our presence.

In our current fear of authoritarianism we have developed a phobia of authority. The political "hero" of my student days was Eugene McCarthy, the ultimate in the nonleader. McCarthy represented the very antithesis of what we saw in the authoritarian style of Lyndon Johnson. But leadership ills will not be cured by having no leaders. If some styles of leadership are inadequate and the self-understanding of some leaders is faulty, then such things can be changed. But we must have leaders. We must learn to exercise legitimately given authority without being authoritarian.

Oddly enough, sometimes there is a kind of incipient clericalism behind our efforts to appear to be non-leaders of the community's worship. By demonstrating our own crisis of identity through our fumbling leadership, our determined effort to appear to be "just one of the boys" who is obviously uncomfortable with this "holy man" image, we call attention to ourselves as if our own self-image were the central issue in ministry. The congregation is saved from having to worship and meet God by our turning the service into a display of our self-doubts, authority questions, and loudly proclaimed sense of inadequacy. The preacher is still the center of the show, a paradigm not of one who is servant of the Word and an official of the community at worship, but

213

one who subtly dominates worship with his or her own personality struggles.

A key factor in whether the liturgy works is the pastor's leadership. The presider of the liturgy sets the tone of the assembly, educates by his very presence and attitude, provides coherence and unity to the community's celebrations, helps move the congregation toward its desired goal, and reminds the congregation under whose grace and judgment we all stand. Whether the worship of the community conveys openness and hospitality, whether the community approaches its meetings with the divine in a spirit of confidence and trust, will be determined to a frighteningly large measure by the nature of its pastoral leadership. While the pastor's self-understanding may not be the primary factor in the pastor's "officialness," the pastor's acceptance of that officialness and disposition toward the demands of that role are of great consequence. If the priest doubts the activity of God in the liturgy, that doubt will express itself in manipulation that seeks to make it happen and that becomes a confession of the absence of God, or paternalism and showmanship in which the priest takes over the liturgy from God, or a kind of halfhearted apathy lay persons detect as basic dishonesty in which their leader goes through the motions but is not personally present. In so doing the priest demeans not only his own presence and potency as an instrument of community and as a sacrament of divine-human meeting, but also demeans the community itself for which the priest is the official. In doubting the importance of his own work in the pulpit and before that altar, the pastor appears to doubt the validity of the community that has commissioned him, doubting that God would ever condescend to work through one so lowly as he to bless a community so inadequate as this.

As Godfrey Diekmann noted, "The Donatists may

have been wrong theologically, but they were pastorally, oh, so right."[15] While the priest is neither the primary actor nor responder in the liturgy, the priest is the primary instrument of action and response. He is the sign of the presence of the entire people of God. And, as Aquinas said of a sacrament, "by signifying it effects." The presiding pastor gives visible expression to the faith and devotion of the congregation and to the graceful community forming work of Christ among his people and thereby becomes an agent of faith and formation. The U.S. Catholic bishops were right when they declared a few years ago, "Good celebration nourishes faith, poor celebration weakens and destroys faith."

Finally, the leader of the liturgy will be most helpful to the community not only when he confidently assumes the role the community has bestowed upon him but also when it is apparent that the one who is preacher in the pulpit and priest before the altar is also pastor to the community. The petty moralizing and scolding that have become the bane of Protestant preaching, both theologically liberal and conservative preaching, seem to occur most often in those situations where the preacher forgets that he or she is also the pastor. "Prophetic" preaching (an insult to the tortured "pastoral" empathy of the Old Testament prophets) is too often used by the preacher as an outlet for whatever unresolved hostility remains from the pastor's own adolescent rebellion against authority. In such preaching, the pastor sets himself or herself at odds with the very community from which the preacher's authorization comes, as if the prophetic word were funneled through the lone spokesman for God to a detached group of which the spokesman is not a member. A truly prophetic word can best be delivered only by the one who stands under the Word in solidarity with the people, who not only preaches from the pulpit but invites and nourishes at the Table. The unity of Word and sacrament is not only theologically desirable but also pastorally essential.

The same can be said for worship leaders who become liturgical dilettantes, "chancel prancers" as Luther called them, officious robots in the liturgy rather than officials of the community. The liturgy is not some pure, unspotted holy entity the ages have handed down to us for aesthetic enjoyment. The liturgy is "the work of the people," it is the action, the yearning, the heartbreak, and the outstretched hands of those who are gathered around the Table and the action, the yearning, the heartbreak, and outstretched hands of the God who deems to meet them in the flesh. The term *pastoral liturgy*, traditionally applied to the study of the practical functioning of the liturgy, is a tautology.

An example of the reciprocal and necessary relationships between the ordained minister's roles of priest and pastor is that Reformed liturgical invention we often refer to as the "pastoral prayer." The "pastoral prayer," which is found in many Baptist, Methodist, and Presbyterian services, is generally an extemporaneous, wide-ranging prayer that is prayed by the pastor during the course of Sunday worship. As far as I am concerned, the "pastoral prayer" is one of the major problems in Protestant worship.[16] I agree with Leander Keck of Yale Divinity School who characterized it as mostly "a bowl of wet, soggy noodles dumped on a helpless congregation." I have two main objections to the pastoral prayers I hear; they are not prayers, and they are usually not very pastoral. Protestant pastors have long been berated for turning their public prayers into sermonettes with the eyes closed, cliché-ridden, vague ramblings prayed at people or about people rather than for people. This is far different than a priestly effort to bring the congregation before God. Prayer may be a problem for

216

many of our people because they so rarely participate in prayer in public worship!

Secondly, "pastoral prayers" are too often abstract, nonspecific, detached, formalized ramblings that sound as if they were prayed by one who is a stranger to the congregation. The extemporaneous, free prayer, prayed by a congregation's pastor can be a significant part of Sunday worship, particularly in those churches that have a tradition of so-called free prayer. But it should be *prayer*; that is, it should be a well-formed, well-stated, properly focused attempt on the part of the pastor to speak and listen to God. It should also be pastoral so that the pastor ought to sound like a specific, knowledgeable, caring person speaking about the specific needs of a specific congregation. The priest has a right to pray on behalf of the congregation on Sunday only if the priest has truly been a pastor Monday through Saturday. The pastor can speak in prayer only if he or she has listened at the bedside, and in the kitchen, and in the counseling session. True liturgical prayer necessitates this kind of pastoral sensitivity, engagement, and solidarity. In-depth pastoral care will inevitably necessitate prayer.[17] I can remember some weeks within my parish when I would approach the "pastoral prayer"—or any other prayer within the liturgy—with a kind of pastoral exhaustion and desperation: "Lord, I have done all that I can do, and they have done all that they can do. Now, in openness, emptiness, and confidence, we come. Hear us when we cry to thee." Prayer within the context of our pastoral counseling (or, for that matter, pastoral counseling within the context of a praying community) may help remind us that people within the community are not obstacles to be overcome or subjects of manipulative church programs or problems to be solved; they are sinful and redeemed children of God who simply want to be heard.

At such times, when the priest dares to boldly and expectantly lead God's people before the throne of grace, I have confidence that such shepherding will not go unrewarded. The people will be blessed through the pastor's leading—perhaps not cured, not improved, or not fully healed. They will be blessed. That blessing will be reward enough for the one who has faithfully led.

Notes

Introduction

1. William H. Willimon, "The Relationship of Liturgical Education to Worship Participation," *Religious Education,* vol. 69 (September-October, 1974), pp. 621-27.

2. Harville Hendrix, "Pastoral Counseling: In Search of a New Paradigm," *Pastoral Psychology,* vol. 25 (Spring, 1977), pp. 157-72, discusses the need for expanded images of who the pastoral counselor is. Hendrix argues that the priest is the dominant image for pastoral counseling, using the term in a broader sense than I use the term. "Prophet" is the image Hendrix believes pastoral counselors should work under.

Chapter 1

1. For instance, James D. Glasse, in listing the criteria for "competence in the ministry," devotes chapters to the pastor as social organizer, counselor, and communicator but gives only a sentence or two to the minister's ability to lead worship. *Putting It Together in the Parish* (Nashville: Abingdon, 1971), pp. 134-35.

2. Paul W. Hoon, *The Integrity of Worship* (Nashville: Abingdon, 1971), pp. 25-27.

3. Ibid., p. 298.

4. Bernard Cooke, *Ministry to Word and Sacraments* (Philadelphia: Fortress Press, 1976), pp. 33-112.

5. Karl Barth, *Church Dogmatics,* trans. G. W. Bromiley, IV/2 (Edinburgh: T & T Clark, 1958), p. 638.

6. James White, *New Forms of Worship* (Nashville: Abingdon, 1971), pp. 32 ff; Don Wardlaw, "Takestock: Worship" (worship workshop by Don Wardlaw, McCormick Seminary, Chicago).

7. John Macquarrie, *Paths in Spirituality* (New York: Harper & Row, 1972), pp. 53 ff.

8. Karl Barth, *Dogmatics*, IV/1, p. 705; *Encyclical Mediator Dei* (November 20, 1947).

9. Frank C. Senn, "Martin Luther's Revision of the Eucharistic Canon in the Formula Missae of 1523," *Concordia Theological Monthly*, vol. 44 (January, 1973), pp. 39 ff.

10. Paul W. Pruyser, *A Dynamic Psychology of Religion* (New York: Harper, 1968), pp. 178-79.

Chapter 2

1. William A. Clebsch and Charles R. Jaeckle, *Pastoral Care in Historical Perspective* (Englewood Cliffs, N.J.: Prentice-Hall, 1964), pp. 34-66. Seward Hiltner, *Preface to Pastoral Theology* (Nashville: Abingdon, 1958), pp. 89-172, first discussed the first three historic functions of pastoral care.

2. Clebsch and Jaeckle, *Pastoral Care,* p. 13.

3. J. A. Jungmann, S.J., *Pastoral Liturgy* (New York: Herder and Herder, 1962), p. 380.

4. Clebsch and Jaeckle, *Pastoral Care,* pp. 124-35; Mary Catherine O'Conner, *The Art of Dying Well: The Development of the Ars Moriendi* (New York: Columbia University Prèss, 1942).

5. Richard Baxter, *The Reformed Pastor,* ed. Hugh Martin (London: SCM Press Ltd., 1956; Richmond, Va.: John Knox Press, 1963), pp. 48-49.

6. It should be noted that Boisen himself stressed corporate care, seeing hospital patients *as a worshiping congregation.* He was uneasy with some of Clinical Pastoral Education's later developments. See Anton Boisen, *Out of the Depths* (Harper, 1960), chap. 5, "An Adventure in Theological Education," pp. 143-97. Boisen also wrote a hymnbook for use in psychiatric hospitals. Anton Boisen, *Lift Up Your Hearts: A Service-Book for Use in Hospitals* (later retitled *Hymns of Hope and Courage* (Philadelphia: Pilgrim Press, 1950).

7. Urban T. Holmes III, *The Future Shape of Ministry* (New York: The Seabury Press, 1971), pp. 173-78.

8. Paul W. Pruyser, *The Minister as Diagnostician* (Philadelphia: The Westminster Press, 1976). See Gaylord B. Noyce, "Has Ministry's Nerve Been Cut by the Pastoral Counseling Movement?" *The Christian Century,* vol. 95 (February 1-8, 1978), pp. 103-14.

9. Pruyser, *Minister as Diagnostician,* p. 43. Pruyser's views on why people seek a *pastoral* counselor are supported by data collected by Emil J. Posavac and Bruce M. Hartung, "An Exploration into the Reasons People Choose a Pastoral Counselor Instead of Another Type of Psychotherapist," *The Journal of Pastoral Care,* vol. 31 (March, 1977), pp. 23-31.

10. Pruyser, "The Use and Neglect of Pastoral Resources," *Pastoral Psychology,* vol. 23 (September, 1972), p. 9. To be fair, Seward Hiltner in his *Pastoral Counseling* (Nashville: Abingdon, 1949), p. 226, listed certain "Religious Resources" that were of help to pastors but

says, "Here, perhaps more than any other area of interest where pastoral counseling is the focus, we need more, and more adequate, reports of actual experience." David K. Switzer, in "Considerations of the Religious Dimensions of Emotional Disorder," *Pastoral Psychology*, vol. 24 (Summer, 1976), p. 327, writes: "Opportunity for worship . . . , may be an especially potent therapeutic process itself. . . . There is no more appropriate setting for the reality testing of religions ideation and delusional systems than a worship service."

11. Pruyser, *Minister as Diagnostician*, p. 48. This was also James Dittes's opinion when he wrote "In Relation to All Psychology," *Pastoral Psychology*, vol. 21 (February, 1970), p. 49. "Pastoral psychology of the next twenty years should encourage the pastor to take far more seriously that which is uniquely and decisively his own basis for his relationships with his people, namely his role as a religious and church leader."

12. Don S. Browning, *The Moral Context of Pastoral Care* (Philadelphia: The Westminster Press, 1976), pp. 108-9. This is much the same issue that Karl Menninger raises in his *Whatever Became of Sin?* Menninger wonders who will confront the problems related to the normative value systems that relate to our everyday life decisions if neither psychiatry nor pastoral care works from a moral context. Menninger's observations are based on his assumption that psychological problems involve value confusions as frequently as they involve emotional and interpersonal dynamics. Care must be given to both value issues and emotional-interpersonal dynamics. Implicit in Menninger and Browning is the idea that the minister must work out of a context where clarification and stabilization of value issues are as prominent as the issues of emotional and interpersonal dynamics. Karl Menninger, *Whatever Became of Sin?* (New York: Hawthorn Books, Inc., 1973). One of my colleagues at Duke, Harmon Smith, raises similar issues with pastoral counselors, but from his perspective of Christian ethics. "Language, Belief, Authority: Crises for Christian Ministry and Professional Identity," *Pastoral Psychology* (April, 1972), pp. 15-21.

13. See Ivan Illich, *Tools for Conviviality* (New York: Harper, 1973), pp. 1-7, and *Medical Nemesis* (New York: Pantheon Press, 1976). Unfortunately, one can expect continued affection for the medical model due to the current efforts of some pastoral counselors to be approved to receive third-party payments from private and governmental sources for their services. See Seward Hiltner, "Pastoral Counseling and the Church," *The Journal of Pastoral Care*, vol. 31 (September, 1977), pp. 202-5.

14. Glenn E. Whitlock, *Preventive Psychology and the Church* (Philadelphia: The Westminster Press, 1973), pp. 16-17.

15. Browning, *The Moral Context*, p. 105. This stress of churchly context puts Browning at odds with many of his pastoral care colleagues. For instance, Wayne E. Oates, after discussing the shift in the pastor's authority from that of "a priestly conveyor of the

sacraments" to "a person equipped and trained" says with a sense of pride:

> "The Protestant pastoral counselor neither depends upon his 'personage' nor the institution of the church for his professional competence as a counselor. . . . The Protestant pastoral counseling movement in America has rightly concentrated much attention and energy upon the development of professionally valid forms of clinical pastoral education . . . accreditation, qualification, and authorization of the pastor as a counselor are of great importance to Protestant theological educators."

Wayne E. Oates, *Protestant Pastoral Counseling* (Philadelphia: The Westminster Press, 1962), p. 161. Seward Hiltner and Lowell G. Colston in *The Context of Pastoral Counseling* (Nashville: Abingdon, 1961) focus on the ecclesial context of pastoral care, but their delineation of the specific nature of that context is unclear, and their reference to the context as a worship community is negligible. I found Hiltner's address, "Pastoral Counseling and the Church," *The Journal of Pastoral Care,* vol. 31 (September, 1977), pp. 194-209, much more sensitive to the contextual importance of pastoral care.

16. In an editorial in *Pastoral Psychology* (February, 1972), pp. 5-6, Charles W. Scott writes:

> "We need to be aware of the close relationship between pastoral care and worship . . . however skilled and empathetic the counselor may be, he cannot in his own person reflect the caring and sharing community that epitomizes worship at its truest. . . . This is not to advocate worship as a counseling 'tool,' for worship is false if it is seen as a means to an end and not an end in itself. But it should not be forgotten that one of the advantages the pastoral counselor has over his secular counterpart is that he works within the context of a worshiping community."

An intriguing example of an attempt to "use" worship in a therapeutic, institutional setting, along with a theologically responsible evaluation of its use, is William R. Philips and Don S. Browning, "A Litany for Thankfulness," *Journal of Pastoral Care,* vol. 27 (March, 1973), pp. 21-25.

17. H. Boone Porter, Jr., "Ministerial Priesthood and Diaconate in Holy Scripture," *Worship,* vol. 51 (July, 1977), pp. 326-31; Bernard Cooke, *Ministry to Word and Sacraments* (Philadelphia: Fortress Press, 1976), pp. 33-57.

Chapter 3

1. Jonathan Edwards, *Religious Affections,* ed. John E. Smith (New Haven: Yale University Press, 1959).

2. Seward Hiltner, *Pastoral Counseling* (Nashville: Abingdon, 1949), pp. 71 ff.

3. Carl Rogers, *Client-Centered Therapy* (New York: Houghton Mifflin Co., 1951), p. 97.

4. Paul W. Pruyser, *A Dynamic Psychology of Religion* (New York: Harper, 1968), pp. 176-78.

5. For example, see Wayne E. Oates, *Protestant Pastoral Counseling* (Philadelphia: The Westminster Press, 1962), pp. 88-91.

6. Pruyser, *Dynamic Psychology,* p. 178.

7. Richard A. Goodling, "The Bible in Pastoral Counseling," *The Duke Divinity School Review,* vol. 41 (Fall, 1976), pp. 178-95.

8. Pruyser, *The Minister as Diagnostician* (Philadelphia: The Westminster Press, 1976), pp. 60-79, 81-82.

9. William Muehl, *All the Damned Angels* (Philadelphia: Pilgrim Press, 1972), pp. 24-31.

Chapter 4

1. Sigmund Freud, *The Future of an Illusion,* trans. W. D. Robson-Scott (New York: Liveright Pub. Corp., 1949).

2. Carl Gustav Jung, *Modern Man in Search of a Soul,* trans. W. S. Dell and C. F. Baynes (New York: Harcourt Brace, and Co., 1936); and *Psychology and Religion* (New Haven: Yale University Press, 1938).

3. See for instance Mircea Eliade's *Images and Symbols,* trans. Philip Mairet (New York: Sheed and Ward, 1962).

4. E. R. Goodenough, *The Psychology of Religious Experiences* (New York: Basic Books, 1965), p. 8; Pruyser, *A Dynamic Psychology of Religion,* pp. 337-39.

5. James E. Dittes, *The Church in the Way* (New York: Charles Scribner's Sons, 1967), pp. 326-50.

6. Ibid., p. 331.

7. Ibid., pp. 337-38.

8. Dittes says that "on the whole, worship does not seem to provide much opportunity for behavioral reflection," ibid., p. 338. I disagree. Since worship is usually visible, active behavior, I see it as a rich opportunity for such reflection.

9. I am indebted to Rodney J. Hunter, "Ministry—or Magic?" *Princeton Seminary Bulletin,* vol. 1 (New Series, 1977), pp. 61-67, for helping me to organize my thoughts on the persistence of resistance and its consequences for ministry.

10. Ibid., p. 65.

Chapter 5

1. Edward Shils, "Ritual and Crisis," in Donald R. Cutler, ed., *The Religious Situation: 1968* (Boston: Beacon Press), p. 736.

2. Jessica Mitford, *The American Way of Death* (New York: Simon and Schuster, 1963); Victor Turner, *The Ritual Process* (Chicago: Aldine Publishing Co., Inc., 1969).

3. Howard J. Clinebell, Jr., "How to Set Up and Lead a Grief Recovery Group," *The Christian Ministry,* vol. 6 (November, 1975), pp. 34-36.

4. Edgar Jackson, *Understanding Grief, Its Roots, Dynamics and Treatment* (Nashville: Abingdon, 1957); Granger Westberg, *Good Grief* (Rock Island, Ill.: Augustana, 1962); David Switzer, *The Dynamics of Grief* (Nashville: Abingdon, 1970), pp. 93-177, details the dynamics of the grief process.

5. Schuyler Brown, "Bereavement in New Testament Perspective," *Worship*, vol. 48 (February, 1974), pp. 93-98. See also Willimon, "Can a Christian Grieve?" *New Covenant* (March, 1978).

6. Janet Eells, "In Time of Grief," *Journal of Religion and Health*, vol. 16 (April, 1977), pp. 116-18.

7. John P. Meier, "Catholic Funerals in the Light of Scripture," *Worship*, vol. 48 (April, 1974), pp. 206-16.

8. This criticism is certainly not true of those modern classics in the literature of the funeral like Paul E. Irion, *The Funeral: Vestige or Value* (Nashville: Abingdon, 1966); Robert W. Bailey, *The Minister and Grief* (New York: Hawthorn Books, 1976); and Austin H. Kutscher, comp., *Religion and Bereavement: Counsel for the Physician, Advice for the Bereaved, Thoughts for the Clergyman* (New York: Health Sciences Pub. Corp., 1972).

9. William Sloan Coffin, Jr., *Once to Every Man and Nation* (New York: Atheneum, 1977), pp. 82-83.

10. See Wilfred Bailey, *Awakened Worship* (Nashville: Abingdon), pp. 136-43, for a funeral statement by one congregation; and C. C. Crawford, "How to Beat the High Cost of Funerals," *The Christian Ministry*, vol. 8 (May, 1977), pp. 26-28.

11. Paul W. Hoon, "Theology, Death and the Funeral Liturgy," *Union Seminary Quarterly Review*, vol. 31 (Spring, 1976), pp. 169-81; Elisabeth Kübler-Ross, *On Death and Dying* (New York: Macmillan, 1969). For criticism of Kübler-Ross's "natural" death views from the standpoint of Christian theology, see Roy Branson, "Is Acceptance a Denial of Death? Another Look at Kübler-Ross," *The Christian Century* (May 7, 1975), pp. 464-68.

Chapter 6

1. John H. Westerhoff and Gwen Kennedy Neville, *Learning Through Liturgy* (New York: Seabury Press, 1978), pp. 91-92.

2. Arnold Van Gennep, *Les Rites de Passage* (Paris: Emile Nourry, 1909).

3. See G. H. Joyce, *Marriage: An Historical and Doctrinal Study* (New York: Sheed and Ward, 1948); and E. Schillebeeckx, *Marriage: Secular and Sacred* (New York: Sheed and Ward, 1965), for historical background on the wedding service.

4. See study by Dr. Theron Neese of Columbia Seminary, Atlanta, Georgia, which is cited in *Informal Conversations with Seward Hiltner: Marriage, Sex, and the Church Today* (Nashville: abingdon audio-graphics, 1975).

5. See W. Norman Pittenger, *Making Sexuality Human* (Philadelphia: United Church Press, 1970); and Stephen Sapp, *Sexuality, the Bible, and Science* (Philadelphia: Fortress Press, 1977), chaps. 1-4.

6. Lawrence A. Cremin, *American Education: The Colonial Experience 1607–1783* (New York: Harper, 1970), p. xiii.

7. For purposes of quotation in the following discussion, I have used the adaptation of *The Book of Common Prayer*'s "Service of Holy Matrimony" which appears in the United Methodist *The Book of*

Worship (Nashville: The Methodist Publishing House, 1964), pp. 28-31. This service was changed very little by Cranmer from its medieval antecedents and is the basis for nearly every traditional Protestant service.

8. See Willimon, *Saying Yes to Marriage: The Two Shall Become One Flesh* (Valley Forge, Pennsylvania: Judson Press, 1979).

9. I fear the possibility that some of the contemporary symbolic accretions the marriage service has acquired in some churches (giving of a rosebud from the bride's bouquet to the mother of the bride, drinking from the "loving cup," lighting of a "Wedding Candle") may obscure the central symbolism of joining hands and exchanging vows by overloading the service with superficial and sentimental liturgical bric-a-brac. The central historic symbols are powerful enough in themselves to adequately express our faith in marriage if we do these symbols well and focus upon them in our education for marriage.

10. While Protestants may argue that marriage is not a sacrament, most of them describe and participate in the service as if they had little doubt that marriage were a primary "means of grace." This indicates that there may be much to be said for James F. White's suggestion that the number of sacraments should again be an "open question" for the church.

11. The so-called Rituals with the Divorced in *Ritual in a New Day* (Nashville: Abingdon, 1976), pp. 74-96, show the problem of conceiving of worship as primarily a therapeutic attempt to meet the needs of people. The result is a questionable accommodation to the values of the culture that may only accentuate people's needs rather than bring the church's resources to bear in ministering to these needs. See my "The Risk of Divorce," *The Christian Century* (June, 1979).

12. For good examples of contemporary attempts to construct marriage services that are more adequate contemporary statements of our faith in marriage, see "The Celebration and Blessing of a Marriage," *The Book of Common Prayer* (New York: The Church Hymnal Corporation, 1977), pp. 422-23, and Hoyt Hickman, ed., *A Service of Christian Marriage* (Nashville: Abingdon, forthcoming).

13. Excerpt from the cassette tape *Informal Conversations with Seward Hiltner: Marriage, Sex, and the Church Today* (Nashville: abingdon audio-graphics, 1975).

Chapter 7

1. Willimon, "A Liberating Word in Water," *The Christian Century* (March 22, 1978), pp. 302-6.

2. G. H. W. Lampe and David M. Paton, eds., *One Lord, One Baptism* (London: SCM Press, 1960), p. 70.

3. James White, *Christian Worship in Transition* (Nashville: Abingdon, 1976), pp. 42-51.

4. *Institutes of the Christian Religion* IV, 14, 3 (Philadelphia: Westminster Press, 1960), II, 1278.

5. Johannes Schneider, *Die Taufe im Neuen Testament* (Stuttgart: Kohlhammer, 1952), p. 30.

6. Robert W. Jenson, "The Mandate and Promise of Baptism," *Interpretation* (July, 1976), pp. 271-87.

7. P. T. Forsyth, *The Church and the Sacraments* (London: Independent Press, Ltd., 1949), pp. 177-78.

8. George McCauley, S.J., *The God of the Group* (Niles, Illinois: Argus Communications, 1975), pp. 23-24.

9. See Lawrence H. Stookey, "Three New Initiation Rites," *Worship* (January, 1977), pp. 33-49; *A Service of Baptism, Confirmation, and Renewal* (Nashville: The United Methodist Publishing House, 1976).

10. Aidan Kavanaugh, O.S.B., in *Made Not Born, New Perspectives on Christian Initiation and the Catechumenate* (Notre Dame: Murphy Center for Liturgical Studies, 1976), p. 133.

11. See Frank C. Senn, *The Pastor as Worship Leader* (Minneapolis: Augsburg, 1977), pp. 64-76, and *A Service of Baptism, Confirmation, and Renewal: Introduction, Text, Commentary, and Instructions* (Nashville: The United Methodist Publishing House, 1976), pp. 17-30, for suggestions for pastoral leadership of the new baptismal rites.

12. Here Luther was simply paraphrasing Romans 6:4 (RSV): "We were buried therefore with him by baptism into death, so that as Christ was raised from the dead by the glory of the Father, we too might walk in newness of life."

13. Richard Jensen, "How Many Baptisms?" *The Lutheran Quarterly* (November, 1975), pp. 312-21.

Chapter 8
1. Paul W. Pruyser, "The Use and Neglect of Pastoral Resources," *Pastoral Psychology* (September, 1972), pp. 5-17.

2. Hans Conzelmann, *An Outline of the Theology of the New Testament*, trans. John Bowden (New York: Harper, 1969), pp. 52-53. Cf. Paul S. Minear, "Paul's Teaching on the Eucharist in First Corinthians," *Worship* (February, 1970), p. 83 ff.

3. Willi Marxsen, *The Lord's Supper as a Christological Problem*, trans. Lorenz Nietung (Philadelphia: Fortress Press, 1970), pp. 34-35. See also Jean-Jacques von Allmen, *The Lord's Supper*, trans. W. Fletcher Fleet (Richmond: John Knox Press, 1969), pp. 14-15; Edward Schillebeeckx, O.P., *The Eucharist* (New York: Sheed and Ward, 1968), p. 123.

4. This claim was made explicitly by Vatican II: "The Eucharist both perfectly signifies and *wonderfully effects* that sharing in God's life and unity of God's people by which the Church exists" (italics mine). *Vatican Council II, The Conciliar and Post Conciliar Documents*, Austin Flannery, O.P., ed. (Collegeville, Minnesota: The Liturgical Press, 1975), p. 107.

5. Peter L. Berger and Thomas Luckmann, *The Social Construction of Reality* (Garden City, N.Y.: Doubleday, 1966), p. 158.

6. Erik Erikson, "The Development of Ritualization," *The Religious*

Situation: 1968, ed. Donald R. Cutler (Boston: Beacon Press, 1968), pp. 711-33.

7. Howard J. Clinebell, Jr., *Basic Types of Pastoral Counseling* (Nashville: Abingdon, 1966), p. 171; Eliot D. Chapple and Carleton Coon, *Principles of Anthropology* (New York: Holt, Rinehart and Winston, 1942), pp. 130-44. There is some debate as to whether our rituals "express" or "effect" experience, whether they merely express our values or form our values. In contending that rituals like the Eucharist help form community, we must admit that one does not engage in such rituals unless one expects or desires, to some extent, the change the ritual promises to effect. Such expectation can be considered a necessary prerequisite for the ritual's effecting quality.

8. Margaretta K. Bowers, *Conflicts in the Clergy* (New York: Thomas Nelson and Sons, 1963), p. 45. See also Howard J. Clinebell, Jr., *Mental Health Through Christian Community* (Nashville: Abingdon, 1965), p. 58. Anton Boisen wrote, "The function of Christian worship is to help men to face their actual problems and difficulties in the light of the Christian faith and to find insight and courage to deal with them constructively." "The Consultation Clinic," *Pastoral Psychology* (March, 1960), pp. 50-51. Cf. Don S. Browning, *The Moral Context of Pastoral Care* (Philadelphia: Westminster Press, 1976), p. 89.

9. William E. Hulme, *Pastoral Care Comes of Age* (Nashville: Abingdon, 1970), p. 85.

10. Suggested by Robert W. Hovda, *Strong, Loving, and Wise* (Washington: The Liturgical Conference, 1976), p. 20. See also Dietrich von Hildebrand, *Liturgy and Personality* (Baltimore: Helicon Press, 1960), chap. 4.

11. Erik Erikson, *Toys and Reasons* (New York: W. W. Norton, 1977), pp. 43 f.

12. See William K. Phipps, "The Kiss of Love," *Pastoral Psychology* (February, 1972), pp. 27-32, for a brief historical survey of the Peace and some psychological observations on reasons for its demise and the need for its recovery in Christian worship.

13. Mary Collins in *It's Your Own Mystery*, Melissa Kay, ed. (Washington: The Liturgical Conference, 1977), p. 9.

14. Paul Tillich, "Theology and Symbolism," *Religious Symbolism*, ed. F. Ernest Johnson (New York: Harper, 1955), p. 108.

15. Augustine, Sermon 272; quoted by J. J. von Allmen, *The Lord's Supper*, trans. W. Fletcher Fleet (Richmond, Virginia: John Knox Press, 1969), p. 60.

16. Collins, *It's Your Own Mystery*, pp. 9-11.

17. Quoted by Bernard Häring, *A Sacramental Spirituality*, trans. R. A. Wilson (New York: Sheed and Ward, 1965), p. 152.

18. I am indebted to George McCauley, S.J., *The God of the Group* (Niles, Illinois: Argus Communications, 1975), p. 75, for this perspective.

19. Augustine, Sermon 272.

Chapter 9

1. Ronald Sleeth, in inquiring into the possible motives behind recent attempts to detract from the importance of preaching (in spite of a large amount of data that suggests its continued centrality), suspects the preacher's self-doubts may be the source of doubts about preaching:

> "Many clergymen today within the Church are questioning the preaching office under the guise of its ineffectiveness communicatively or its authoritarian theological claims when the real problem is the preaching office in relation to their own being. . . . Preaching reveals their own internality, and this can be a terrible threat. They are not sure of their own being and are terrified by the resultant insecurities of faith and personality that such exposure as preaching unveils. . . . They do not want to preach for they fear the revelation of their innermost selves."

Ronald E. Sleeth, "The Crisis in Preaching," *Perkins Journal*, vol. 30 (Summer, 1977), p. 11.

2. George McCauley, S.J., *The God of the Group* (Niles, Illinois: Argus Communications, 1975), p. 84. I am deeply indebted to Father McCauley's book for helping me to organize my thoughts on ordination. While I approach the subject somewhat anthropologically and therefore functionally, as does Father McCauley, I believe that my conclusions are not at odds with historical and theological scholarship on the subject. For an excellent survey of that scholarship, see Bernard Cooke, *Ministry to Word and Sacrament* (Philadelphia: Fortress Press, 1976), mentioned in chap. 1.

3. Henri Nouwen, *The Wounded Healer: Ministry in Contemporary Society* (Garden City, N.Y.: Doubleday, 1972); Urban T. Holmes, *The Future Shape of Ministry* (New York: The Seabury Press, 1971), pp. 27, 31. In a recent book on ministry, Holmes goes on to claim special intuitive, imaginative powers for the clergy, *Ministry and Imagination* (New York: The Seabury Press, 1976), chap. 9. See also Holmes, *The Priest in Community* (New York: The Seabury Press, 1978).

4. Seward Hiltner, *Ferment in the Ministry* (Nashville: Abingdon, 1969), p. 58; Lyle E. Schaller, *The Change Agent* (Nashville: Abingdon, 1972), and *Parish Planning* (Nashville: Abingdon, 1971).

5. James D. Glasse, *Profession: Minister* (Nashville: Abingdon, 1968). See also David C. Jacobson, *The Positive Use of the Minister's Role* (Philadelphia: The Westminster Press, 1967), pp. 21-22. In the face of criticism of clerical "professionalism," Glasse appears to be modifying his earlier position somewhat. See "Beyond Professionalism," *The Christian Ministry* (March, 1978), pp. 12-14.

6. Richard John Neuhaus, "Freedom for Ministry," *The Christian Century* (February 2-9, 1977), p. 86.

7. McCauley, *God of the Group*, p. 86.

8. Georges Bernanos, *The Diary of a Country Priest* (Garden City, N.Y.: Doubleday, 1954), pp. 22-23.

9. McCauley, *God of the Group*, p. 87.

10. Earlier, Gibson Winter noted how pastoral counseling's fondness for one-to-one caring relationships often obscured the pastoral function of the church as a fellowship and turned clergy away from their community-building function. "Pastoral Counseling or Pastoral Care," *Pastoral Psychology*, vol. 8 (February, 1957), pp. 16-22.

11. McCauley, *God of the Group*, p. 88.

12. Ibid., p. 89.

13. Paul W. Pruyser, "The Master Hand: Psychological Notes on Pastoral Blessing," William B. Oglesby, Jr., ed., *The New Shape of Pastoral Theology: Essays in Honor of Seward Hiltner* (Nashville: Abingdon, 1969), pp. 352-65.

14. Ibid., p. 361.

15. Godfrey Diekmann, O.S.B., in the introduction to Robert Hovda, *Strong, Loving, and Wise: Presiding in the Liturgy* (Washington, D.C.: The Liturgical Conference, 1976), p. vi. Father Hovda's book is an excellent discussion on the theological rationale and the practical specifics for presiding in the liturgy.

16. R. P. Marshall, "The Pastoral Prayer in Today's Worship," *Religion in Life*, vol. 43 (Autumn, 1974), pp. 192-96.

17. See William E. Hulme, *Pastoral Care Comes of Age* (Nashville: Abingdon, 1970), pp. 151 ff., for a discussion of the value of personal prayer in pastoral care.

Scripture Index

Subject Index

232